CH00822472

BUILDING SENSORIMOTOR SYSTEMS IN CHILDREN WITH DEVELOPMENTAL TRAUMA

by the same author

**Improving Sensory Processing in
Traumatized Children**
Practical Ideas to Help Your Child's Movement,
Coordination and Body Awareness
ISBN 978 1 78592 004 2
eISBN 978 1 78450 239 3

of related interest

The Handbook of Therapeutic Care for Children
Evidence-Informed Approaches to Working with Traumatized
Children and Adolescents in Foster, Kinship and Adoptive Care
Edited by Janise Mitchell, Joe Tucci and Ed Tronick
Foreword by Stephen W. Porges
ISBN 978 1 78592 751 5
eISBN 978 1 78450 554 7

**Attachment-Based Milieus for Healing Child and
Adolescent Developmental Trauma**
A Relational Approach for Use in Settings from Inpatient
Psychiatry to Special Education Classrooms
John Stewart
Foreword by Dan Hughes
ISBN 978 1 78592 789 8
eISBN 978 1 78450 739 8
Paperback ISBN 978 1 78592 790 4

**Using Stories to Build Bridges with
Traumatized Children**
Creative Ideas for Therapy, Life Story Work,
Direct Work and Parenting
Kim S. Golding
ISBN 978 1 84905 540 6
ISBN 978 0 85700 961 6

**Life Story Therapy with
Traumatized Children**
A Model for Practice
Richard Rose
ISBN 978 1 84905 272 6
eISBN 978 0 85700 574 8

BUILDING SENSORIMOTOR SYSTEMS IN CHILDREN WITH DEVELOPMENTAL TRAUMA

A Model for Practice

SARAH LLOYD

Illustrated by Liv Rose Whitfield

Foreword by Brian Rock

Jessica Kingsley Publishers
London and Philadelphia

First published in 2020
by Jessica Kingsley Publishers
73 Collier Street
London N1 9BE, UK
and
400 Market Street, Suite 400
Philadelphia, PA 19106, USA

www.jkp.com

Copyright © Sarah Lloyd 2020
Foreword copyright © Brian Rock 2020
Illustrations copyright © Liv Rose Whitfield 2020

All rights reserved. No part of this publication may be reproduced in any material form (including photocopying, storing in any medium by electronic means or transmitting) without the written permission of the copyright owner except in accordance with the provisions of the law or under terms of a licence issued in the UK by the Copyright Licensing Agency Ltd. www.cla.co.uk or in overseas territories by the relevant reproduction rights organization, for details see www.ifrro.org. Applications for the copyright owner's written permission to reproduce any part of this publication should be addressed to the publisher.

Warning: The doing of an unauthorised act in relation to a copyright work may result in both a civil claim for damages and criminal prosecution.

Library of Congress Cataloging in Publication Data
A CIP catalog record for this book is available from the Library of Congress

British Library Cataloguing in Publication Data
A CIP catalogue record for this book is available from the British Library

ISBN 978 1 78592 629 7
eISBN 978 1 78592 630 3

Printed and bound in Great Britain

Contents

Foreword

I HAVE known about the pioneering dedication of Sarah Lloyd for several years and the outstanding outcomes she has been achieving through the application of her BUSS model developed over many years of significant experience with children, young people, families, carers and professional networks.

Sarah's background as an occupational therapist combined with decades of experience working in child and adolescent mental health services (CAMHS) brings an unusual depth of thinking and feeling to the model's underpinnings and application. This captures a key element of Sarah's approach; she is, in the best sense of the word, an integrationist. She brings concepts and ideas together, drawing on what appears to be antithetical traditions, in the service of providing an accessible and effective set of interventions that makes a real difference to people's lives. Here there is much innovation and development for which we should be grateful.

There is a richness to Sarah's ideas as well as a simplicity that belies the decades of thinking and experience she brings. One can almost be forgiven for thinking 'Why didn't I think of that?' In fact, Sarah's commitment is to a group of children and young people – Looked After Children – who, because of early adverse experiences, including trauma, neglect and significant loss, have not had the (relational) experiences required to foster the development and mastery of their own bodies that makes it more difficult for them to feel confident, engage in their world, be it at home or school, and ultimately hinder their life chances. This book sets out an approach for parents, carers and teachers to address the lack of opportunities for children in practical ways that enable them to restore what has been absent from their early childhoods.

She achieves something unusual and extraordinary in this book and indeed in her previous book, too – you 'hear' her voice, her passion and her clarity in the words you read; her work comes alive. Sarah has a talent for understanding and conveying the essence of particularly the children and young people she works with. It is a very particular group she has dedicated herself to help even though the model no doubt has wider applicability.

Reading Sarah's work – as indeed is the case when meeting her – one is struck by her humility and her immense perseverance and determination. She is on a mission to share her work to benefit others, test her theory and practice and ultimately develop a wider network of people to offer these interventions to support families and shift the balance from practice-based evidence to evidence-based practice through further research.

Brian Rock
Director of Education and Training and
Dean of Postgraduate Studies
The Tavistock and Portman
NHS Foundation Trust

Acknowledgements

I 'M very fond of that expression, 'it takes a village to raise a child' and I feel so grateful to the very many people who have helped me get to the end of this book!

A huge thank you to all of the children, young people, parents, foster carers, special guardians and kinship carers whom I've worked with over the years. I've learned so much from you all and it's been a privilege to be part of your lives for a short time. A special thank you to the gym club parents, who have done such a brilliant job of talking to so many people about the Building Underdeveloped Sensorimotor Systems (BUSS) model. I love our Friday mornings, thank you.

I feel really lucky to have worked in so many great teams in my career so far, and to have learned so much and had the opportunities to develop my practice. The BUSS model wouldn't be where it is today without the help and support of Lorian Rein and Helen Tait (at the Oakdale Centre), Katie Wrench in the Therapeutic Social Work Team, and Shelagh Ethell at One Adoption West Yorkshire. You've all been so instrumental in how we've developed the model and I look forward to many more years of collaboration. There's a great culture of innovation in Leeds at the moment and I'm so glad to have had the chance to work with people and teams that I couldn't have without the support of Jane Mischenko, our brilliant Children's Commissioner. Thanks too to Adoption Plus; Joanne Alper and her team are doing great work and it's been a treat to work with Yvonne Milton and Jo Hart and have other occupational therapist heads to think with!

Thank you to the many parents, carers and colleagues who helped shape this manuscript – I have to mention Phil, who ploughed through it over and over again! Thanks Vicky, Sarah,

Harriet, Lindsey, Lynette, Kate, Paula, Emma and Susie for your encouragement and helpful comments (and Susie for your patience with grammar – without you there would have been a lot of very long sentences and endless dashes!).

I'm delighted to have met Liv, who has done the illustrations for this book. It's been an absolute pleasure to work with you and I love your work.

Thank you, Stephen Jones at JKP, for asking me to write another book. I really appreciated your insights into the world of publishing and the very helpful, practical advice you gave me. If anyone is thinking of writing a book in this kind of field, Stephen is a great person to talk to about it – he knows so much.

And in the good tradition of saving the best until last – none of this would have been possible without the love and support of my family. Thank you, Ray, for your love and confidence in me, as well as picking up a lot of the boring jobs over the last year to give me time to write. To our children, Ally and Kirsten, who have been so positive and supportive of me doing this – we could not be prouder of the young women you are both growing into. And to my parents, without your love and care I'd never have been in a place to start on any of this. Thank you all!

Introduction

I T'S easy for us, as grown-ups, to forget the wonder of our bodies as efficient machines or finely tuned instruments. In an age of increasing technological advances, we have yet to discover anything as efficient as the human body, with its ability to fight disease, its built-in recharge system, and the simple joy that is to be had from moving. My favourite book is Ann Patchett's (2017) brilliant fictional work, *Run* (appropriately about adoption!) and in it she gives the most beautifully vivid description of the pure, unadulterated pleasure that Kenya, the child in the book, gets from running. She describes the exhilaration, the execution of the moves and the reaction it elicits among the bystanders in a way that is at the same time humbling and can't fail to excite and reawaken awe in our bodies and what we can do. If you watch young children as they first discover and then strive to get their bodies to do what they're wanting them to do, we see that same excitement as they learn to crawl, walk, run, hop, skip, run round in circles, whirl themselves round and round until they're completely dizzy, slide down slides, forwards, backwards, on their bottoms, on their tummies , swing on swings, do handstands, hang upside down on bars, climb trees, go sledging – all the most simple of pleasures. We can do these things because we know our bodies and they (generally) do what we want and need them to do.

Unless you have, or have had, a disability, or you're a person for whom it's a particular area of work or study, we don't, as a rule, spend much time thinking about how this comes about. Watching children move from one stage of development to another, we might marvel in the process but we don't really question how it is that children can make the transition from crawling to walking or handstands to cartwheels. The process by which we grow into ourselves on a bodily level is an almost all-consuming part of our early lives and yet it's a relatively neglected area of study when we think about children and young people who have experienced early adversity. And this is what has fascinated me – how can we have got so good at understanding the psychological impact of early abuse and deprivation but almost completely forgotten about our bodies.

As a student occupational therapist (OT) back in the 1980s, I knew that I wanted to work in children's mental health services and I feel lucky to have spent most of my career there. I was fortunate to get a great foundation in psychodynamic understanding and clinical work through a training scheme run by the Department of Psychotherapy in Leeds in the 1990s. This led to me doing, among other things, a master's degree in psychoanalytic studies, a clinical training in play therapy, and further training to become an eye movement desensitization and reprocessing (EMDR) practitioner.

It's been a great time to work in children's mental health services. I've been privileged to have worked in child and adolescent mental health services (CAMHS), both in Leeds and Fife, with colleagues who have been keen to build skills and understanding of the impact of early experiences on the developing child. When I was working in Fife CAMHS (2005–2013) there was the opportunity to be part of a CAMHS/social care team (the Springfield Project), developing therapeutic services for children who were looked after. We began offering a range of different psychological therapies and had a range of expertise – including child psychotherapy, child psychology, social work and art therapy – that allowed us to offer consultation to colleagues in social work and CAMHS, support for foster carers, and assessment and direct work with children. This was the first time in my career that I had not had a very mixed caseload (previous posts had typically been split between different clinical teams) and working exclusively with children with developmental trauma really shaped my understanding of the impact of early adversity on all aspects of development. I began to notice a significant group of children and young people who weren't making the kind of progress in therapy we'd expected, and whose movements seemed floppier and more out of synch with themselves than I'd previously noticed. They might trip walking along the (completely straight and obstacle-free) corridors or slide along the walls. They were sometimes quite frenetic, crashing and banging around in a way that never seemed to tire them. Their heads were often down, looking at the floor, and I began to rethink the kind of disengagement I'd previously understood as psychological resistance, wanting to better understand how they were functioning on a bodily level. Was their head drooped because they were feeling sad and didn't want to be here, or was their head drooping because they had really weak muscles around the head, neck and shoulder girdle?

I turned to sensory integration therapy for help in understanding what was happening, but only found partial answers. Sensory integration is defined as, 'an innate neurobiological process and refers to the integration and interpretation of sensory stimulation from the environment by the brain' (Hatch-Rasmussen in Koscinski 2017, p.20). Sensory integration theory was first described by Jean Ayres (1972) and sensory integration therapy is based on this theory and designed to help people with problems in sensory processing disorder.[1] The mainstream texts were all about children with sensory processing disorders and, for me, didn't talk enough about trauma or what state of mind a child might be in or the relationships around that child. This mirrored my experience of most of the literature around trauma and children in care, which tended to focus on relationships and state of mind, but didn't say much about bodily awareness and functioning.

I decided to become better informed about the theory behind sensory integration and did the first level of the training available to OTs and physiotherapists. I was enthused by what I heard – sensory integration theory helpfully mapped all the different pathways that early movement experiences lay down and I began to understand the neurophysiology of how babies and children in loving, nurturing environments grow into themselves on a bodily level through repeated experiences of loving care and stimulation. It was from here that I developed the Building Underdeveloped Sensorimotor Systems (BUSS) model, based on the understanding that early adversity means that, while babies and young children

---

1   www.sensoryintegration.org.uk

have missed out on good, nurturing relationships, it's likely that their bodies have also missed the sorts of movements that go hand in hand with those relationships. Babies who feel safe and happy do lots of moving and have lots of good experiences of touch and nurture. Babies in frightening situations (in utero and once they're born) don't have these same touch experiences; and because they're not thriving and being stimulated, they don't move nearly as much as typically developing children and as such their systems can be compromised. These systems are what help us to feel grounded and connected to the earth; they mean that we have good head, neck and shoulder strength as well as a strong core. Our movements are generally fairly smooth and well coordinated and we might use our eyes to look where we're going, but we don't have to watch our feet when we're coming down some stairs or our hands when we're writing to check they're doing the right thing.

I'm now back in Leeds and I'm working from Leeds CAMHS on a secondment to the Therapeutic Social Work Team (who work with children in foster care and kinship placements) and One Adoption West Yorkshire (who work with adoptive families). I feel incredibly lucky to be in these great teams, working with some amazing families, and to have the opportunity to develop the BUSS model across the lifespan of children who are, or who have been, looked after. There are lots of interesting projects on the go, including a programme with the Therapeutic Team and the Virtual School, looking at school readiness in a group of four-year-olds who are in foster or kinship/connected care and due to be starting school soon, as well as work with foster carers and babies, and babies and family finding teams. All great teams and really exciting work.

The BUSS model

This model is designed to bridge a gap that I found existed in how we support children and families who have experienced early adversity. It's not a standalone model, but is intended to sit alongside the models that helpfully support families – the great work of the

ChildTrauma Academy[2] and Bruce Perry's neurosequential model (2006) (we'll revisit his hierarchy of regulate, relate, reason many times in this book); attachment theory and the understanding that we develop in the context of relationship – the baby brain developing alongside the adult brain (Gerhardt 2004, reprinted 2014; Malloch and Trevarthen 2004; Music 2011; Stern 1985; Trevarthen Delafield-Butt and Dunlop 2018; Winnicott 1957; Zeedyk 2011); the work of Dan Hughes and Kim Golding (2012); the advances in child development (Sharma and Cockerill 2014a and 2014b) and our understanding of how children learn (Conkbayir 2017; Stewart 2011; Tredgett 2015).

The BUSS model adds to these an understanding of how a baby and young child's sense of themselves on a bodily level develops as they move within nurturing relationships. Drawing on sensory integration theory, the model takes as its starting point the understanding that without nurturing relationships babies don't progress through the stages of movement that are needed to feed the brain and central nervous system with enough information to build an internal map of the body and lay the foundation for well-coordinated movement. The BUSS model advocates the potential of rebuilding the gaps in these systems, using games and activities that take place within relationships that offer the child a loving, attuned base to grow from.

As you'll read throughout this book, going back and redoing essential patterns of movement that were missed has a significant effect on a child's sense of themselves on a bodily level and how much more in synch with themselves and coordinated they are. This means that children are able to go from being the person who wasn't able to join in with games and activities that required skills like running, skipping, rapid changes of direction, or upper body strength, to being able to enjoy the kinds of physical games and activities that are such an important part of childhood.

When I started to develop the BUSS model, I'd imagined that once a child was more in tune with themselves on a bodily level, the next step would be psychological therapies, supporting their emotional and relational development. What surprised me was that

---

2   http://childtrauma.org

it seemed to have an impact not only on their bodily regulation but also on their emotional and psychological well-being. One parent said that she'd always been a bit puzzled that professionals were always asking her about eye contact and whether her daughter had good eye contact. She said that after doing the BUSS intervention, she suddenly understood what they meant – her daughter had started looking at her in a way that felt more than just a glance in her direction as she was dashing off to do something else; it was a look that had more connection to it. Her daughter was much calmer and they would sit and chat and play together in a way that they had never been able to before.

Other parents talk about how much less angry their child becomes, and often describe their child as seeming much more comfortable in their own body. It's interesting to think about how frustrating it must be for children who have to fight against their bodies to move around and do things, and it is little wonder that they seem tense and angry. The amount of energy and effort that this takes is phenomenal, and what's lovely to hear, as children grow into themselves on a bodily level, is how much more energy and capacity they have.

This can sometimes come as a surprise to parents. One father emailed me a month after we'd finished working together to say that he'd just been to a parents' evening and heard that his child had suddenly started working much better in the class. Concentration and focus had improved and, for the first time, the child had written a whole story – and it was beautifully written. This dad had always assumed that his daughter had some sort of learning difficulty and so had never really pushed her in terms of school. I suspect that it was more that she was having to use so much of her mind to focus on movement and getting through the day that there was no spare capacity for learning. How wonderful to be freed up and have some space for other things to grow!

You'll read, in Chapter 17, the account from Nadia's mum of how her daughter started being able to manage things like waiting and not always having to be first, how she started being able to share, take turns and that her friendships at school really blossomed. Amber's mum talks about how her daughter was able to start making friends and going out; Lenny's mum discusses how he was able to manage after-school clubs and football practice. All of these are huge gains in emotional regulation and relationships, and it's just fantastic to see how an intervention that focuses so much on bodily regulation can really progress these things. I guess we shouldn't be surprised, because it's just what happens in typical development – babies grow into themselves on a bodily level within a nurturing relationship, before they even have language. If you're someone who quite likes to know how things end, then do feel free to begin by reading the parents' accounts in Chapter 17.

What I'm hoping this book will do

This book has two purposes. If you're a practitioner (and I use the word 'practitioner' to include anyone who works in a professional relationship with children, in a social care, education or health setting), I want to interest you in the way children learn to move and offer a lens to begin to notice how a child is moving. From there, I'd like to give you a framework for understanding what you're seeing and the extent to which this may or may not fit with an underdeveloped system. I hope that the ways of working and activities I talk about will give you ideas for supporting families to begin to rebuild their child's underdeveloped systems. I also hope that you'll want to learn more and see the BUSS model as a useful addition to the skills that you already have.

If you're a parent or carer, I want to give you enough information to help you to think about whether the BUSS model might be helpful for your child and, if it is, to get you started. As parents and carers, you have expert knowledge of your own child and can make informed decisions, based on a wealth of information, as to how best to work with them, what's normal for them, what they enjoy, what motivates them and so on. So you might feel that you want to experiment with suggestions in this book or you might want to do more training or find an accredited BUSS practitioner to support you in that journey.

This book talks about using the BUSS model with school age children, but the practice is different and was way beyond the scope of the book.

There are different levels of training on the BUSS model available for practitioners, schools, parents and carers. For more information please go to our website www.BUSSmodel.org.

What this book won't do

This model can be helpful with a certain population – children whose early experiences mean that they've missed out on the loving, secure, nurturing environment that allows them to grow into themselves on an emotional and physical level. This model is not designed for children whose early experiences have been good enough, even if the way they move or present might look a bit like a child with an underdeveloped system – this is much more likely to be a sensory processing disorder, a distinction we'll come on to in the next chapter. And alongside that come a few other caveats. While I'll be encouraging you to look at a child who has experienced early adversity and wonder whether their foundation sensorimotor systems are functioning as well as they can be, don't lose sight of the fact that any child might become unwell and that we're all our own unique, individual selves. So while I'm always really hopeful of being able improve a child's level of functioning, if I notice things like them losing areas of function or skills that they've previously had, I want them to see a paediatrician fairly swiftly. And while I might see a child who has suffered abuse and neglect as a baby and who has a diagnosis of autism, I am clear that although I might be able to help with the bodily regulation that's about an underdeveloped system, it's not going to make the autism go away. But for any child, feeling more comfortable in their own skin and not having to use up so much energy managing their body frees up a bit of capacity for other things, so I hope that it would help somewhere!

This book is not a treatment manual. While there is a stepped progression to a lot of the activities, it's not a matter of starting at the bottom and working your way up through the stages. Getting the right activities and the right starting points for individual children will vary, depending on the interplay of their experiences and circumstances and how these have impacted on the development of their foundation systems. I hope that sharing my experience of working with children and families using this model, and parents talking about how they've found it, will help to build your understanding of what this model is about and how it might be helpful.

Don't get mixed up between this model and sensory integration therapy

Sensory integration therapy aims to treat the functional deficit, whereas BUSS aims to go back and fill in the gaps in the foundation systems so that there isn't a deficit. Sensory integration therapy (often called Ayres' sensory integration therapy) has been developed for work with children with a sensory processing disorder – and that is quite different from an underdeveloped system. In a sensory processing disorder (like developmental coordination delay or the sort of sensory profile you might see in someone with a diagnosis of autism spectrum disorder), the child will typically have had very 'normal' early experiences – grown up in loving, nurturing families and had opportunities for relationships and movements – and the difficulties lie with the way the information is coming into or being transmitted from the brain and central nervous system. So it's not a question of there not having been enough input or information to adequately feed and prime the system, rather that something goes wrong in the way the information is both processed and then transmitted.

How the book progresses

I'll start by introducing the foundation systems, helping you to tune in to how a child is moving and considering if this is the right intervention and right time for this kind of model. I'll then take you through the assessment process that I have developed, illustrating this with case examples. Some of these children and families will appear throughout the book, others will appear more briefly to illustrate a particular point. Once I've taken you through each part of the assessment and given consideration to how you make sense of what's happening, we'll look at ideas that I've found useful in supporting families and schools in rebuilding the underdeveloped parts of the child's foundation systems.

The final part of the book is given over to parents for them to tell you their experiences of using this model with their children. I'm so grateful to them for their willingness to share their experiences and hope that you find it helpful.

Chapter 1

Introducing the Foundation Systems

T HERE'S something quite mind-blowing about the human brain and the potential that babies are born with. Bruce Perry (2006) describes the infinite potential and huge vulnerability of the infant brain: while it can be fed and shaped with sensitive care, it can be terribly damaged by abuse and neglect. We are all born with our unique genetic code but how it plays out depends on our experiences, which influence the brain's architecture as we grow. Those early relationships literally determine the way the brain develops in response to experience. And the rate of growth is phenomenal – between two months and two years, synapses (which carry neural impulses between cells) are produced at the rate of 1.8 million per second (Lane and Schaaf 2010). Such big numbers can seem overwhelming but can give some perspective on the importance of those first two years of life when the brain is being formed and shaped. The brain changes throughout our lives (this is often referred to as the plasticity of the brain) but never as much as in these first two years.

It's this balance of physical care and emotional nurture that is the hallmark of good care in the early years. If we think of a tiny, hungry baby crying – they have no understanding of why they feel the way they do, and what they need is someone not only to feed them but also to soothe them and help them know that everything is going to be alright; what they're feeling is because they're hungry and it will all be better once they've had some food. If we only did one aspect of this – either the nurture or the meeting of the physiological needs – the baby wouldn't thrive and might not even survive; it's this interplay of care and helping the baby to make sense of themselves and their bodies that is one of the huge tasks in the first year of life.

I nurse an idea that I might have an as yet untapped capacity to play the piano. I know that there must be some genetic potential there (at least to get so far) but unless I first learn and then practise there is no way I'm going to even get started. However, it would be impossible for me to become a great pianist without access to a piano. It's just the same with babies and growing into themselves on a bodily level. They need a consistent, loving relationship to be doing the moving and exploring that come naturally as part of that.

Babies move all the time when they're interested or stimulated by a person or environment. When I'm training I often show a clip of a very small baby lying on a mat and the 'conversation' they are having with their parent. When I first started training I used to ask my audience to tell me what they noticed from this interaction. They all noticed important things about the relationship – the eye contact, the mirroring, the attunement, the reciprocity, all of which are undoubtedly there. But no one ever noticed what was happening from the head down – all of those huge arm and leg movements that the baby was doing within that interaction. These movements are so important! But babies only do all this moving when they feel safe and happy, initially in relation to adults who are attuned and available to them. So, if we really can't separate out moving and relationships in typical development, we need to keep them together when we're rebuilding systems too.

Without the kinds of movements that happen within the context of love and care, the baby's brain and central nervous system isn't fed with enough information for them to develop good bodily regulation. It's a very active process and a baby needs to be doing lots of moving, playing and interacting for them to grow into themselves on a bodily level. For this they need an attuned adult alongside them. It's a bit like when you're trying to persuade yourself to do some exercise – I find that lying in bed I can visualize my whole morning run but unless I actually get out of bed and go do it, I'm not going to get any better at it.

The foundation systems

These systems are so called because, as you'll see, they literally provide the foundations from which we grow into ourselves on a bodily level. Understanding how our systems develop in 'good enough' environments gives us the blueprint to work from when we're trying to understand the gaps in the movement vocabularies of children with developmental trauma. I'll give a brief overview of each of the systems before we think in greater depth in later chapters about their development and how we might start to build them if they're underdeveloped.

The vestibular system

The receptors for our vestibular system are in our inner ears. As we'll think more about in Chapter 9, they're tiny hair-like structures that are stimulated by movements of our heads. These movements set off a series of events in our brain and central nervous systems that contribute to a sense of balance and spatial awareness. If our body was a crane, the vestibular system would be like the base of that crane. It helps us to feel grounded and gives a stable base for moving. On a bodily level, our base (or core) is our head, neck, shoulder girdle and trunk. The vestibular system has two main tasks. The first is to provide core strength and stability to our bodies. The second is what's called gravitational security – helping us to feel secure in our movements, being able to go down steps or jump up and down without it feeling precarious or as if the ground is moving with us.

The vestibular system is designed to begin its development in utero, and then, once the baby has been born, is always at work in response to gravity and movement. But we know that when babies are in frightening environments they tend to freeze rather than move freely. Babies need to feel safe and contained to move and flourish in relation to their caregiver.

Children with underdeveloped vestibular systems will often have poor posture and low muscle tone – they'll feel a bit saggy in the middle and might slide along walls or have poor balance and coordination. There might be a fearfulness about movement

(you can often notice this when you watch a child going down a flight of stairs) or lots of sensory-seeking behaviour – crashing, banging, whizzing around. None of us likes to look foolish or as if we can't do things as well as the next person, and it's just the same for children. I find that children often use speed to make up for a lack of control and you might only notice how this system is working when you ask them to slow down.

The proprioceptive system

This is all about the smooth, well-coordinated working of muscle groups. In this system, the messages travel from the muscles and joints up to the brain and central nervous system and back down to the muscles and joints, telling us how much pressure, force, strength and so on to use in a movement.

Our proprioceptive systems are always working to give us information about where our bodies are in relation to our environment. You can try this by just closing your eyes and reaching out for something that you know is in front of you, like a drink. You shouldn't need to use your eyes to find your drink and you don't have to think about how to pick it up. Your brain will have been working hard without you being consciously aware of what it's doing, mapping out your environment, alerting you to things you need to know about, deciding what you don't need to be consciously aware of. If you stop briefly and really tune in to all the noises that are around you, you'll see how much your brain has been filtering out, so you can focus on what you're wanting to do without constantly being distracted. It's just the same on a bodily level. Good proprioception is knowing what your body is doing without having to use your eyes to track or plan how your body is going to move or work – how much pressure or force to use in a movement. When you bend down from your chair to pick something up off the floor, you're not having to think about how far to lean forwards or how to stop yourself toppling forwards onto the floor; your body knows how much pressure or force is required for the movement.

We sometimes become aware of this if something unexpected happens. I was in an old building recently, which I hadn't been to before. It was only when I found myself falling through the door as I opened it that I realized that my brain must have taken in the old surroundings and assumed that it was going to be a big, old, heavy door, so I pushed really hard, only to find that it was a new door painted to look like an old door, so the amount of pressure or force needed to open it was completely different and I fell into the room. (Embarrassingly, this was my introductory session for a pilates class – not the entrance I'd been hoping to make!)

A child whose proprioceptive system is underdeveloped might struggle to know where the different parts of their body are (older children sometimes talk about not knowing what their feet are doing unless they can see them). If you don't really have a sense of where your body is from the muscles and joints inside your body, a good way to find out is to move around a lot, or bump into things, and so we often see a lot of extra movement in children with underdeveloped proprioceptive systems. Movements are often poorly modulated and are either too floppy or too jerky. Sometimes I think that this inability to modulate pressure or force is a bit like trying to water a delicate pot plant with a power hose, or fill an enormous bath with a dripping tap – really tricky.

Like all of our foundation systems, the proprioceptive system grows through repeated patterns of movement when a child is feeling safe and happy. Think of a baby learning to crawl, all those times when they are up on all fours and then rocking backwards and forwards as their muscles and joints prepare for the movement – all of those movements are vital in developing bodily awareness. We can see the baby's hands flat on the floor, their wrists moving as they rock, their body getting used to being off the ground, supporting itself, their eyes getting used to judging distance, their body working out how much pressure/force to use. When you watch a young child at this stage of development, when they're moving from creeping on their tummy to crawling, you see lots of trial and error, lots of overshooting the movements or not using enough pressure and collapsing back down. All of this builds up an internal map about the position of their body and what they need to do to be moving around.

The tactile system

This develops from one that is primed for survival in the newborn baby, when all the receptors are alert to danger and function to protect the baby from harm. With nurture, love and care, the system shifts from this defensive functioning to discriminatory functioning. As the baby no longer needs to be constantly looking out for danger  because someone else is taking care of them, the receptors change so that instead of being alert to danger, they allow the child to begin to discern what they're touching. This shift allows the developing child to stay tuned in to the moment of an experience and explore, rather than being preoccupied with protection and safety. Early feeding experiences are an important part of the tactile system and we'll think about this much more in Chapter 5. Children who have experienced abuse and neglect are often stuck in a defensive mode and their systems are on high alert.

The limbic system

 The limbic system is a group of structures that sit, quite literally, in the middle of our brain. I remember, a long time ago, being in the audience when Bruce Perry was describing the structures of the limbic system. He encouraged us all to get a £1 note out, fold it up and put it into our hands, making a fist around it. This, he told us, was just how the limbic systems sits, nestled in the middle of the brain. I thought that was such a helpful way of beginning to understand such a complex set of structures!

The limbic system operates on an unconscious level, and it can be helpful to think of it as the music that constantly plays in the background. It's the unconscious process that sets our state of mind – flight/fight/freeze, or a state of mind that allows us to stay in the moment of an experience, be able to manage the uncertainty of not knowing or letting someone else be in charge of things. It's in this second state of mind that we make and store memories and experiences in a way that they can be usefully retrieved when we're under stress. Children need to feel safe and happy to start to play or learn; they need to be able to stay in the moment of an experience and tolerate uncertainty or not knowing everything.

These systems are underdeveloped, not broken

Understanding how the foundation systems typically develop and viewing them as underdeveloped rather than broken in children who have experienced early abuse and neglect underpins the BUSS model. This allows us to take the child back through essential patterns of movements that have been missed, within the context of the safe and nurturing environment that foster carers or adoptive parents are able to offer. This can help to relay these foundations, rebuilding the child's sense of themselves on a bodily level. It gives a critical platform for emotion regulation, building relationships and learning. Bruce Perry's (2016) neurosequential model talks about the pyramid of the three Rs – Regulation is at the bottom, the middle tier is Relate and the top tier is Reason. If that foundation layer of bodily and emotional regulation isn't solidly established, it can be much harder for the subsequent layers to develop – a bit like trying to put a roof on a house without having finished the walls.

We can sometimes get a glimpse of what this might be like if we think of a time when we were injured or hurt ourselves. Having a part of our body that isn't working well or is giving a lot of pain can become quite preoccupying. Suddenly, activities that we've done without thinking, like walking down a flight of stairs or getting into a car, become huge mountains to be climbed as we try to work out the least painful way to move ourselves from one place to another. While I'm not suggesting that children with underdeveloped systems are in pain, I do think that they have to expend an enormous amount of attention and energy on trying to get their bodies to do what they want them to do. Once children have done some work to get their bodies more in synch with themselves, rebuilding those foundation systems, they often talk about how much less tired they feel. Parents notice their humour more or the child being more chatty, as if the burden of having to move their body around lessens and there is more energy and capacity for other things: relating, playing, exploring, learning, moving and getting pleasure from it. It's hard for us to imagine what that must be like for children, though Raghu sums it up beautifully.

RAGHU: THE JOY OF MOVING

Raghu is a six-year-old boy who I worked with to rebuild his foundation systems. His early life had been very neglectful and had left him completely out of synch with himself on a bodily level. He often fell over, always seemed to be bumping into things, never seemed to be able to gauge how much pressure or force to use when he was doing something and so would often crash into his friends when he was just meaning to give them a hug. He was struggling with sitting still, writing and learning at school, and at home didn't seem able to absorb the great opportunities and loving relationships that were available to him.

His family worked really hard over a couple of months to rebuild vestibular, proprioceptive and tactile functioning and I was delighted to get an email from his mum to tell me about a conversation she'd had with Raghu. He had been running up and down the stairs over and over again and when she asked him why he was doing that, he turned round, gave her a huge grin, spread his arms wide and said, 'Because I can!'

Development as a top-down process

Typically developing children get control from the head down, so their head, neck, shoulder girdle and trunk develop before they get much control of their legs. Think of a six-month-old baby sitting in a highchair – they can sit up with only a little support and are learning how to control their arms and their hands as they reach for things or feed themselves. But if we were to

take this six-month-old out of their highchair and stand them up, they would just sit straight down, because while their head, neck, shoulder girdle and trunk are all developing as they should, their lower limbs are still relatively weak and underdeveloped. This is just as it should be; for typically developing children, control happens from the head down and each stage gives a good foundation for the development of the next stage. All those early moments like tummy time, rolling over, pushing up, commando crawling, crawling, and cruising set the stage for walking, then running, jumping skipping and hopping, before children learn to do things like hanging upside-down from bars or doing handstands and cartwheels. However neglectful a child's early environment has been, they'll usually stand and then walk at some stage, but if this hasn't followed the normal sequential pattern of movement the child is often left with gaps in their development – and it's these gaps that the BUSS model suggests we can go back and fill in.

Children who have experienced early abuse and neglect often have trouble getting their bodies to work in a well-synchronized way. The upper body and legs seem quite out of time with each other, which gets in the way of smooth, well-coordinated movement. Other children struggle to have their arms working as a helpful part of the movement when they're doing something like running. So while a child might be able to run or dribble a football, if you look at their whole body there won't be a fluidity or synchronicity between the leg and arm movements. I watched a boy jumping from cushion to cushion recently, and, while his legs and feet knew exactly what to do, his upper body was really floppy and his arms were trailing behind him in a way that made it hard for him to complete the movement unless he did it at top speed. For other children, it may be that they struggle to know how much pressure to use when writing, or have to watch their hand very carefully when carrying a glass of water so as not to spill or drop it.

Why is it important – what difference does it make?

Working with children whose foundation systems are underdeveloped makes me realize just how hard they have to work all the time just to get their bodies doing what they want them to do. Usually, we don't even have to pay attention to what we want our bodies to do – we can just do it. We don't have to consciously think through our movements; as we're reaching for a cup, we're not thinking about the flexor and extensor muscles in our arm and how they're going to contract and co-contract – we've got a veritable library of motor programmes stored in our brain and central nervous system so that these familiar activities don't have to come up to a conscious level. When I asked you to try and tune in to the background noise around you in the brief introduction to the proprioceptive section earlier in this chapter, I was wanting to show you how much of that discernment of our environment happens at brainstem level – things don't even come in to our conscious awareness as our brain and central nervous system process and filter them out. Sometimes, if we try and learn a new skill, perhaps learning a dance or trying a new sport, we can experience that disconnect between what our brain is visualizing us doing and what we're actually doing, and sometimes after we've done it we can feel our body hurting in ways it doesn't normally. But generally we can relax and know that our body can take care of things.

When we're thinking about children and young people who don't have this same easy, fluid relationship with their bodies, we need to understand typical child development so that we can get better at noticing gaps in development that are due to an underdeveloped system.

Chapter 2

Beginning to Notice Movement

IT can be hard to take a step back and be objective when you're watching your own child and trying to notice some of the things we've been thinking about, like how comfortable they feel in their own body, and how they're moving. Or to be a practitioner who is used to looking at things from a psychological or relational perspective, to begin to try and notice what's happening on a bodily level for a child. When I'm training practitioners in using the BUSS model, I always encourage them to start with typically developing children rather than the child they feel concerned about. If your professional training didn't involve a lot of child development, or perhaps if you're an adoptive parent who just hasn't spent much time with babies, I'd suggest supplementing your knowledge with additional study around this. To begin with, just getting into the habit of scrutinizing how children are moving and playing is so helpful – even if this is as you're standing in a park or play area or sitting in a soft-play area. I encourage people just to watch how children move and how the different parts of their bodies are working together.

It's time for some action!

It can also be useful to use our own bodies as a starting point. Sometimes we can feel very self-conscious slowing down and watching ourselves doing things that we usually do without engaging our conscious brain, but when we're thinking about systems that are underdeveloped, it's important to have a good appreciation of what typical movement is. Also, because this is a very active kind of intervention, you need to know how it feels as a preliminary step before supporting children and parents as they try to do the different things.

We used to play a game called 'Misfits' when I was growing up (when I tell my now teenage children about it, they roll their eyes and quote my overused explanation of all things that happened before they were born – simpler times!). It was an uncomplicated little card game where there were lots of people and animals divided into heads, bodies and legs, and the fun was to be had in mixing them up – so you could have the head of a ballerina, the body of an astronaut and the legs of a gorilla. Hours of fun! But I often find myself thinking about it as I'm watching children move, trying to understand the interplay of their different systems and parts of their bodies. Try it yourself – just get into that idea of sectioning the body off and seeing what each part is doing before building it up again into a whole body.

It's a good idea to start with a very familiar activity like walking – you probably move in a fairly fluid way, your right arm and left leg move forwards together, and you manage to make progress without falling over or bumping into things. If you're in a place where you can just get up and walk around now, notice how you do it, think about where your head is, how your arms move, what the rhythm is like. Notice what your feet are doing. You should be doing what's known as a 'heel strike, toe peel movement' – you probably do this automatically and have never really thought about it, but just notice it now. Your heel should be the first part of your foot to touch the floor, then the sole of your foot goes along the floor and your toes are the last part of your foot to leave the floor. Walk towards a mirror and watch the position of your arms and legs. It's most efficient to walk so that your right leg and left arm move at the same time, then your right leg and left arm. This is easiest to notice if you speed up a bit, so you're walking pretty fast. Now try walking around moving the arm and leg on the same side together, so your right arm and right leg and left arm and left leg are moving at the same time – notice how different this feels. Then imagine you've got almost no core strength, so your middle is really floppy. What does your body do to compensate for such a wobbly middle? Now try speeding up. What happens?

And then, to make it even more tricky, walk around for a bit and see what happens if you bend down to pick something up, or notice something out of the corner of your eye – how does your body change what it's doing? Now try and pick something up and carry it while you're walking – what happens now? Do you find yourself stooping over or is your body able to maintain a nice stable frame?

You'll be glad to know you can sit down again now!

This should help as you begin to build up a picture of how the child you are thinking about is moving. We'll go into a lot more detail, but to begin with I'd suggest that you just watch them as they're walking:

- What does it look like?

- What is their head position?

- What are their arms doing?

- Does it look fluid and well coordinated?

- Is it smooth or jerky?

- Where are they getting their stability from?

- Are they stamping down very heavily?

- Are their legs bending as they move, or staying stiff?

- Are they walking on tiptoes?

- Where is their eye line?

- Are they watching their body or where they're going?

- Are they bumping into things?

There are so many things you can be noticing! Then put this alongside what you noticed about how you walk. Try and mimic the child's walk and see what you notice. Does it feel the same sort of movement or is it very different? Now go back to walking the way you walk and feel the difference. What was different? Was it how your arms moved? Which leg moved with which arm? Was there something about how stiff or floppy it felt? Did it feel secure or precarious?

Do the same thing with sitting down at a table. Again, if you can, just try it now – stand up and then sit down again. What do you notice? Where is the power coming from for the movement? Where are you getting your stability from? Did you lean on anything as you were sitting? If you did, try again, this time just using your body. What felt different? What did you notice? Did you put your hand on a table or the side of the sofa to steady yourself? If you can, try it again and don't put your hand down – and just notice how it feels.

Then notice how the child you're thinking about sits down at the table – and put this against how you would expect them do it. Generally, what you'd expect to see is the child pull the chair out, sit themselves down on it – so sitting down in a controlled way without flopping down or missing the chair, and without needing to support their body on another surface while they sit down. Then I'd expect the child to use their arms to move the chair into a position that is comfortable for them.

LEROY: WHY NOTICING *HOW* RATHER THAN *WHAT* A CHILD IS DOING CAN BE HELPFUL

Sometimes it's very easy to spot what is different about how a child with an underdeveloped system moves because, while the child might get to the same end point, their route of getting there is very different. I watched a young boy, Leroy, sit down at a table outside recently. Leroy was two years old and I'd been playing with him and his foster carer in his garden, noticing just how often he fell over and how much difficulty he was having shovelling sand into a bucket – he kept overshooting the movement, using so much force that the sand would go flying everywhere and he'd often knock the bucket out of his hand. When it was time for lunch, his foster carer put a sandwich down on the little table in the garden. There was a child-sized chair, with arms, pushed in under the table and I was expecting Leroy to pull the chair out, sit down and then pull his chair back under the table. Instead, he did a very elaborate manoeuvre which involved his legs doing all the work and his arms playing absolutely no part in proceedings. He balanced himself (quite precariously) on one leg while he swung his other leg up into the chair. So at this point, he had one leg on the seat of the chair and one leg on the ground, straddling the arm of the chair. He then managed to very quickly pull his leg that was on the ground up over the arm of the chair and effectively fall into the seat of the chair.

I was quite impressed while at the same time thinking how much work we could do here – no arm involvement or core stability! Later that afternoon I spent a happy hour teaching Leroy and his foster carer to commando crawl, encouraging his arms and shoulders to become an integrated, helpful part of the movement. This is where books can come in handy; something like *The Very Hungry Caterpillar* (Carle 1994) is perfect to read and then re-enact, and in that afternoon with Leroy we were caterpillars, worms, creeping cats – you name it – anything that could possibly be said to move around on their tummy!

Useful resources

There are some great books, programmes and websites around to help to build up a baseline of what typical development looks like in the first five years to supplement direct observation, and I've listed several of these at the end of this book. Used judiciously, the internet and YouTube are treasure troves of videos of children at different stages of development. There have been some great TV programmes in the last few years that examine the lives of babies, two-, three- and four-year-olds (*The Secret Life of...Year Olds*[1]) and again these offer material for building up a sense of what normal development looks like and the variations within that.

---

1   www.channel4.com/programmes/the-secret-life-of-4-and-5year-olds

Getting an idea of whether BUSS is the right model to be using

We're going to go through each of the systems in more detail and talk about how to notice whether they're underdeveloped or not. As I mentioned in the introduction, there are screening tools available, like the *Sensory Profile* (Dunn 2014), but these are written to identify children with a sensory processing disorder, not children whose early experiences mean that they haven't had the nurture or the movement that would allow them to grow into themselves on a bodily level. So as you can imagine, the information from one of these can be quite confusing. Much of the time, a child with an underdeveloped system might have things in common with a child with a sensory processing disorder, but equally they might not, and because what's driving the difficulties is different, their scoring on the sensory profile doesn't offer information at a level that is sensitive enough to helpfully inform or direct an intervention.

If I go into schools and there has been a child in a class who's had a sensory processing disorder, there is often equipment around that was used for that child, such as chew toys, wobble cushions or slanted writing boards. It can sometimes be a challenge to help staff understand that just because the two might look similar in some ways, the intervention and goals should be quite different. When I'm working with a child whose system is underdeveloped, I want to rebuild the child's systems so that they do not need to chew on things, are able sit in a regular chair and have good enough core and shoulder strength and stability to write on a flat surface rather than having to be scaffolded by aids or adaptations.

What if there are other explanations for the difficulties?

I often work with families where the child has already accrued a fair number of diagnoses – neurodevelopmental difficulties like attention deficit hyperactivity disorder (ADHD), autism spectrum disorder (ASD) or developmental delay. I've also met children in wheelchairs because their muscle tone is low and, while there may be an idea somewhere in the system that this is because of the child's early experiences, there is often a gap between this and knowing how to start rebuilding things. I never make any promises about what this intervention might do or shift in these cases, but I do work with these families and generally encourage parents to have a try, in the spirit of thinking that it can do no harm and at the very least we can exclude it as an explanation for the difficulties.

The more I know about child development and the impact of early trauma on the developing brain, the more I want to try and build capacity in children who have had these experiences. For me, the miracle is the child who is able to function on a bodily level after those kinds of experiences. How anyone can emerge from some of the situations children have endured with any sense of which way is up is incredible. Unless a child who has experienced developmental trauma has had an intervention that takes as its starting point the possibility that their systems might be underdeveloped as a result of their experiences, then I always want to give that a shot before turning to a more medical model for an explanation of the difficulties or challenges they might be facing.

Is this the right timing for this intervention?

In developmental terms, the earlier we can get started, the better! It's during those first two years that the architecture of the brain is really being established so if it's at all possible, I like to start working with foster carers and adoptive parents as soon as babies and young children come into their care.

Of course, this isn't always possible, and if a system is under-developed then it's usually possible to improve functioning whatever the age of the child. But we also need to be mindful of the capacity of the parents and carers and what else is happening for them at that time. This is an intervention that can be really effective if there are lots of repetitions of the games and activities, but none of the systems will grow without this practice, so we need to make sure that there is a bit of capacity in the family system.

For me, the BUSS programme is a bit like starting a jigsaw: getting the corner pieces and some of the edge pieces into place to give a frame for the rest of the puzzle to grow into. If we extend the analogy a bit further, to do a jigsaw we need to have a table (or another hard surface) to do it on – there needs to be room on the table to move the pieces around, place pieces next to each other and see whether they might go here, or there. If the table is only just big enough to fit the finished puzzle on, it's going to be much harder to do. So if we think of the child's parents and carers as being like the table, then there needs to be a bit of spare capacity to give the intervention the room it needs – it can't be competing with too many other things. (One of my own children is doing her GCSEs and is using the kitchen table for her revision and there's stiff competition every mealtime to find space for us all to sit at the table without completely disrupting the piles of papers and books.)

If parents or carers are so worn out and frazzled that they're only just getting through the day, then they need more help and support before starting something like this. It's a bit like thinking of the floor the table is standing on. It's very hard to do a jigsaw if the floor is really uneven and the table really wobbly. So we need to make sure that there's enough support around the parents for them to feel they've got the space, time and energy before we get started.

How long will it take to work?

This is always a difficult question to answer; it's very hard to predict how quickly it will be possible to grow the underdeveloped parts of these foundation systems. From my clinical work, I'd say that in any group of ten children that I'm working with, four will make really fast progress, and I'd expect to see things looking significantly better and for me to be feeling that they no longer need my input, within eight weeks of starting. Another four will be making good progress but it will be slower. These are often the children who have had in utero exposure to drugs and alcohol and whose systems just need more support to get them there, and who will probably need to continue to do some work over the next weeks and months to hold on to the gains they've made. The last couple of children may be the ones whose parents have had other things going on so haven't really been able to get started with the intervention (real life does have a habit of getting in the way of the best of intentions!) or are the children whose levels of anxiety are just so high that it's going to take a lot of work just to get them to feel safe enough to begin to try something new. These are the children and families I might work with in a more hands-on way, meeting them every week or linking them with other parents and carers who have experience in using the model and who can 'mentor' them. I also think that families in this situation can benefit from using this intervention alongside something like developmental dyadic psychotherapy (DDP)[2] or Theraplay®,[3] where the therapist supports the parents in getting the level of challenge just right and stays with the tactile system until the child has internalized a sense of well-being and that the things they're going to do are going to be okay.

2 Developmental dyadic psychotherapy is a therapy, parenting approach and model for practice that uses what we know about attachment and developmental trauma to help children and families with their relationships. http://ddpnetwork.org

3 Theraplay® is building strong families and emotionally healthy children and adults through Theraplay® training, treatment, advocacy and research. http://theraplay.org

Chapter 3

The Sequential Nature of Motor Development

BEFORE we get started with how the BUSS model works, and now that you're beginning to think about, and notice, movement, I'd like to take you right back to the beginnings of movement. There is a popular myth that suggests that the faster a baby progresses through (or jumps over) the early stages of development, the smarter and more talented they'll turn out to be. You rarely hear parents boast that their 13-month-old child is still crawling, but if a child is walking 'early', then we're often fooled into thinking that it is a sign of advanced development. But really, each stage is important in its own right, and it's helpful to understand something of the purpose of the many stages that come before crawling and walking. As we know, even when they've had the most deprived start in life, nearly all young children walk, so it's good to think in more detail about the stages and their purpose in the progression towards locomotion.

The developmental process of a baby/young child is phenomenal and quite awe-inspiring. From the perspective of the BUSS model, it is important to be thinking about development starting at conception rather than when a baby is born. Understanding how the baby's time in the womb (intrauterine environment) impacts on their development, as well as getting an understanding of some of the primitive reflexes and the sorts of movement experiences that typically allow them to integrate, is particularly useful when working with foster carers and adoptive parents who have known the child from birth and sometimes struggle to understand how their foundation systems can be compromised (*Note* – There are always different bodies of thought on things, including

THE SEQUENTIAL NATURE OF MOTOR DEVELOPMENT

retained reflexes. Generally, primitive reflexes give way to function (Kosanski 2017) and so we don't normally pay much attention to them. In this book, I'll talk about some primitive reflexes and how they become integrated in typically developing children. From my clinical experience, I find that taking children back through the stages of development that they've missed allows this process of integration to happen, but if someone has concerns, there are some helpful pointers in books like Kathy Brown's *Educate Your Brain: Use Mind–Body Balance to Learn Faster, Work Smarter and Move Through Life More Easily* [Brown 2012].)

I want to highlight the stages that it is most helpful to understand when working with children who've experienced early adversity. We'll return to these stages many times in this book, so it's good to get a firm grasp of them early on. If you're a professional whose training hasn't involved as much detail around children's physical development and you're interested in developing your knowledge about this early stage, then the Sharma and Cockerill (2014a and 2014b) series, based on Mary Sheridan's work with young children, is really useful, especially the online videos that it gives access to. Then there are some brilliant websites by paediatric OTs that are very accessible and give lovely explanations of the stages of development, often with short clips and pictures. Thinking about this first year of life, I recommend CandoKiddo[1] (developed by Rachel Coley) and MamaOT.[2] Christie Kiley, author of the MamaOT website, references the Hawaii Early Learning Profile (HELP), developed by Stephanie Parks (1994). This isn't a standardized assessment tool, but I think it can be helpful because it's done in collaboration with parents based on observations of children in their own environment. For those interested in education, Sharon Tredgett (2015) helpfully links these early movements and the practicalities for the child of being in the learning environment of the classroom. The Boxall Profile, which is widely used in education in the UK, is another very helpful tool for thinking about the different domains of early childhood development.

---

1   www.candokiddo.com
2   https://mamaOT.com

The guidelines that I offer here for expected ages of development use a combination of HELP (Parks 1994), Cockerill and Sharma (2014a and 2014b), Ayres (2005) and DeGangi (2000), as well as information gleaned from training courses like the sensory integration training I did in 2012 with the Sensory Integration Network and with Sensory Babies in 2018.[3]

Development of the baby in utero (in the womb)

For our purpose, we're particularly interested in things that stop a baby moving around in the womb as much and as freely as they should, such as the impact of alcohol and stress. Research and ideas about the impact of drug and alcohol use during pregnancy are changing and the website of FASD (Foetal Alcohol Spectrum Disorder) Network UK[4] is a good place to look for up-to-date information. What we do know is how sensitive the baby is to the stress levels of the mother. There are some really interesting clips on YouTube of babies in utero that it might be helpful to watch as you're thinking about this stage of development. These seem to change or be taken down very frequently so, rather than giving a link, I'd suggest searching for quite specific stages, like '20-week-old baby in utero', as a starting point.

There are a couple of primitive reflexes that are present in utero and that it is helpful to be aware of.

- The *fear paralysis reflex* emerges around 5–7 weeks and is the precursor to the Moro startle reflex. In utero, when stressed, the baby becomes very still, just as the name suggests. If the intrauterine environment is broadly good enough and the baby is more often in a state of well-being rather than feeling stressed, then this reflex integrates by around 32 weeks in utero.

- The *tonic labyrinthine reflex* (TLR) is present from around 12 weeks and what we see is that as the baby moves their head forwards, their body curls in on itself and as they move their head back their body stretches out (extension),

---

3   www.sensoryintegration.org
4   www.fasdnetwork.org

beginning that pattern of developing through movement. This is thought to have been helpful as the baby moves down the birth canal.

Once the baby has been born, there are a number of primitive reflexes that are designed to ensure the baby's survival. Reflexes are innate, automatic movements existing from the time we are in utero onwards. Some are active for only a short period of our lives and others, like blinking, are with us throughout our lives. The following reflexes should give way to function over the first six months of the baby's life.

- The *asymmetric tonic neck reflex* means that when the baby is lying on their back, as they turn their head to one side (perhaps to look at something or someone who 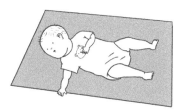 has caught their attention) the limbs on their face side extend and the limbs on their head side flex. This reflex is present from the baby being in utero and should integrate at around four to six months if the baby is spending time on their tummy. This is a brilliant reflex on so many levels, but not least because, when you're lying down beside a baby, it feels as if the baby is turning themselves towards you and reaching out to touch you – all so clever in terms of eliciting a good caregiving response!

- The *rooting and sucking reflex* helps with early feeding patterns and we can see this clearly in the newborn – if you touch the cheek of a young baby near the corner of their mouth they'll turn their head and try to suck your finger. We can see why this is important for survival in those early days and months; without food the baby won't survive, and the newborn's systems are primed to ensure their best chance of survival. Again, with lots of good nurture and care, this fades by six months.

- The *Moro reflex* (often known as the startle reflex). You can normally see this if someone is holding a baby but something changes and the baby's head drops so they don't feel themselves to be well enough supported and have a feeling of falling – their arms will open out wide and then come back together, making a kind of embracing movement. Again, with repeated experiences of good enough care then this too fades by six months.

- The *palmar grasp relfex*. A newborn baby's hands are normally closed, but they do have a strong *palmar grasp*, so that if you rub your finger over their open palm, their fingers will close. Where a baby is growing in a safe and nurturing environment, this fades over the first four to five months of life.

The developing baby

In a lot of ways, it is much easier to think about development once the baby has been born, not least because we can see it all happening! I can't stress enough the context – babies moving within relationships. Even though we're going to go through the stages of development in quite a clinical way, it's really important to keep remembering that this kind of progression will only be happening if the baby has the kind of relationships around them that mean they're feeling safe and happy.

The newborn baby

Let's start with a full-term, newborn baby. Lying on their back, the newborn will usually have their head to one side or the other. When they move, we can see that their arm and leg movements are quite jerky and arms and legs tend to move together. Things move fairly quickly from here and already by three  months the baby generally prefers to hold their head in the midline.

It's lovely to watch babies of this age 'chatting' to friendly and familiar people and, when they're lying on their backs to do this, their arm and leg movements are getting smoother and less jerky.

The beginnings of tummy time

By two to three months, generally babies can be persuaded to spend a bit of time on their tummies. Sometimes they prefer to be propped up a little on a cushion or lying on their tummies on their parents' or carers' knees, just getting used to being in that position. Before they are about two months old, their lack of head control means that they can't lift their face off the floor, which, understandably most babies often find uncomfortable. But by two to three months, as their head control develops, the baby becomes more comfortable on their tummy. You can watch them lifting their head and moving it from side to side without bobbing up and down.

Babies are often beginning to start to experiment with rolling around this time, and rolling is a brilliant way of babies building their core stability. If you can, just try this yourself – lie down on the floor on your back with your body in a straight line, and try and roll yourself over until you're on your tummy and then right over onto your back. You should really feel your abdominal muscles working! If you used your legs or arms to 'power' the movement, just do it again and try and keep them really still.

The first stage of rolling is usually for babies to roll from their side onto their back (around two months), then roll from their tummy to their back (two to five months) before they can roll from being on their back to being on their tummy (six to eight months). The MamaOT website has lots of interesting information about this stage of development, as well as tips about how to make it fun for babies!

Back to babies being on their tummies – by around four months, the baby can support their weight on their forearms while lying on their tummy. Thinking about the next stage of tummy time, by four to six months the baby can bear weight on their hands and push their entire tummy off the ground. This is really the beginning of a different viewpoint and perspective on the world!

From here, by six to seven-and-a-half months, when they're lying on their tummy, the baby can push their chest off the floor using both hands, then shift weight from one hand to another to reach out and get a toy. This facilitates the integration of the asymmetric tonic neck reflex, as the baby gains  control of pushing up from their tummy. This integration allows the baby to play in the midline, having their toys and focus in front

 of them rather than to the side. This is a helpful thing to be noticing when working with young children – as we'll think more about when we're thinking about vestibular and proprioceptive functioning.

I often meet two- and three-year-olds who might look as if they're sitting on the floor playing nicely with, for example, their cars, but when I look more closely I can see that they are only playing with them on one side of their body, never in front of them, and there's no crossing over of the car from one side to the other. With these children, it's helpful to bring them back through the tummy time progression, to facilitate activities that involve crossing the midline of  their body, which is vital in order to have both sides of the brain working together.

Another important development at around this six- to eight-month time (but not on their tummy) is protective extension. When a baby is sitting on their bottom (not supported by anything like a seat back) and they start to wobble forwards or sideways (perhaps reaching for a toy or something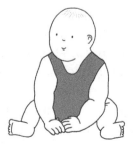

that's taken their interest), then the arm on that side straightens and the baby puts their hand on the floor to catch themselves before they topple over. This is a really helpful protective response, and works when the baby wobbles to the side or forwards. It's interesting that it doesn't come into play if a baby wobbles backwards, and I wonder if that's because evolution is focused on the next stage of development, literally wanting babies to move on to being on their tummies in a crawling position, ready to go and explore. But that's just my idea!

You can see how babies can miss out on these important stages if they're not having the opportunities they need to move and explore. If a baby doesn't spend time on their tummy, then they don't build such good head control and don't get their shoulders and arms working as well. Without time sitting unsupported (so babies always being in little chairs that support them, like car seats or those moulded chairs that hold them in position) they'll never do that wobbling and almost tipping over that stimulates the protective extension response. And that response is really important, not only at this stage of being a baby, but as children start to grow and are walking. We need that protective extension to be well honed so that when they start to fall over they'll be able to instinctively put their arm out to break their fall, rather than falling down onto their faces.

Getting ready for crawling

There's a stage before crawling that is often called creeping, when babies can move themselves forwards on their tummies, using their arms to power the movement. This is a fantastically important stage and you can see just how strong head, shoulders and trunk are at this point. Babies often start by using their arms together in this movement, but can build up good speed by using alternating arms. As you'll see as you go through this book, this is a stage of development that we come back to again and again, so if it's possible to watch typically developing children at this stage, it's really helpful.

In terms of how all of this leads towards crawling, by the time they're six to eight months, a baby lying on their tummy will be beginning to involve their legs in the movement – they can usually reach one knee forwards, bending it towards the trunk. The progression towards crawling is given a fantastic boost around this time (generally six to nine months) by the emergence of the *symmetrical tonic neck reflex* – also known as the crawling reflex. From their position on their tummy, as the baby lifts their head, their arms straighten and push into the floor and their hips and knees flex so they can bear weight on their knees. This helps to get the baby off the ground and ready for action. This reflex also works in the opposite direction. The symmetrical tonic neck reflex should integrate at around 11 months when it's no longer needed to help the baby start to crawl.

If we think about all of this pre-crawling preparation, we can see that by eight to nine months the baby can independently support their weight on their hands and knees. They can rock back to front, side to side, and diagonally. This is  important in preparing the wrist to move in all directions and stimulating the finger extension. By this time, they can often scoot forwards a few feet by moving their arms and legs and are generally delighted with themselves that they can do this!

So by nine months, the typically developing baby is now able to be on their hands and knees and shift their weight from one hand to the other while reaching out, without dropping their tummy to the floor. They're only a tiny way from actually crawling and if we look for a moment at a baby in this position we can see great head strength and control, strong shoulders, lovely straight arms, flat hands with fingers facing forwards – they're ready to be off!

And then they crawl – the dizzy heights of locomotion! They can move at speed and, for most babies, this is the stage before walking. But don't let's rush forwards; if we just think about the advances a child makes through crawling for a moment, we can see many good reasons why it would be useful to go back and fill in gaps in development if children have missed this (and earlier) stages. Christie Kiley of MamaOT describes the main benefits of crawling at this stage and in the box below I've used her basic structure to summarize those and think of the implications for children who have not gone through these developmental stages at the normal time.

MOTOR SKILLS

- Crawling gives the infant one of their first chances to hold their body off the floor and to have their hand flat on the floor, with their fingers facing forwards. This hand position helps with lengthening the long finger muscles that are so important in fine motor tasks, like handwriting. When I'm watching older children crawl, where their early lives have meant that they haven't gone through this lovely sequential process of development, I often notice that their hands are clenched as they crawl. It's really helpful to know that typically developing babies don't crawl like that, except perhaps in the early days. Where we're taking children back through stages of development that have been missed, and wanting to get the maximum benefits from crawling, we need their hands to be in the right position: flat hands, fingers facing forwards.

- Crawling with hands in this position develops the arches of the hand. The arches help the hand to form correctly around objects when we hold something. This is so important in being able to feel and manipulate things with our hands. Being able to mould our hands around an object is an important foundation for throwing and catching as well doing things like holding cutlery or beginning to draw with a crayon. I notice that children who have missed out on these early experiences often use their fingertips to feel things and don't get nearly as much information from this as their bodies are needing to help them make sense of what they're touching or to have a good grasp of it.

- The baby's hand being in this position (flat hands, fingers facing forwards) is really helpful in the process of specialization. We don't need our whole hands to be able to do the same things, and even at this early stage of development, our brain and central nervous system are constantly refining things so that our bodies become more efficient and effective. For the hands, the ulnar side (the side of the small finger) becomes the stabilizer, the radial side (the side of the thumb) the working side – again, crucial for any fine work like handwriting.

- Crawling demands that the baby uses both sides of their body together (bilateral integration and sequencing). As the right hand goes forwards, the left leg moves; then as the left hand goes forwards, the right leg moves. This massively strengthens the connections between the left and right sides of the brain and is so important in our bodies being able to work as one unit, in an integrated way.

- Crawling is also hugely beneficial for developing what is called proximal joint stability – strengthening the joints close to our core, our shoulders and hips. If a child is to have control over their hand and wrist in writing, throwing, catching or even knowing how much pressure or force to use when picking up an object, their body needs a stable base at the shoulders and hips. Crawling is the perfect way to develop this.

- Crawling also helps the baby to develop postural control. We need to be able to hold our bodies in a good upright and stable position for just about everything, from sitting to standing, walking to skipping. A really important building block towards postural control is what's called co-contraction, where different parts of the body work helpfully together with other parts so that it can work as one integrated unit. To be able to crawl, the baby needs to contract all the muscles around their trunk to hold that nice and still while their arms and legs are moving their body forwards. Again, crawling is the perfect chance to do this!

SENSORY ADVANCES

- Although we're focusing on motor development, lots of other changes are happening, including the baby's eyes and whole visual system. When the baby is crawling, they're doing lots of different things with their eyes – looking from hand to hand as they move forwards, tracking where they're going. This ability to visually track from left to right and right to left is important not only at the crawling stage, but throughout our lives. Without this, children often only read one half of a page of text.

- As well as tracking their movement from side to side, the baby is also negotiating their environment. They are looking at where they are and where they might be wanting to go. This develops binocular vision and depth and space perception. Again, these are crucial skills that we need throughout our lives – not just as children sitting in classrooms needing to look up at the board and then back down at our paper, but as adults, when making decisions, for example planning whether to overtake when we're driving.

- As the baby gets better at crawling, they spend more and more time in this all-fours position. This means that the muscles around the baby's trunk are getting stronger, which is very helpful for the development of the internal structures related to breathing, talking and eating.

DALE: A CAUTIONARY TALE OF 'GOOD ENOUGH'

It is important here to revisit the idea of 'good enough' early experiences and the sort of relationships and environments babies need to thrive. It can be easy to fall into the trap of thinking that if a baby has been in foster care, then they will have had good enough experiences, but sadly that's not always the case. I met Dale recently, who was 18 weeks old and had been in foster care for eight weeks. I'd met him when he was 12 weeks old, when he'd only been with his carers for a couple of weeks, and at that stage I noticed how stressed he seemed. His foster carers were lovely, warm, caring and experienced in fostering. I noticed that he was sitting on his carer's knee in a very upright position and his head was constantly turning from one side to the other. His carers thought that he liked seeing the lights and was looking towards them, but I didn't think that was so likely (I thought he was looking for a face to fix on) and we talked about turning him round so that he was looking at them rather than facing outwards, and them using their face and voice to try and soothe him.

When I met him again six weeks later, I was keen to see how things had progressed and we spent some time with him lying on his back. His foster carer and I lay beside him and I encouraged his foster carer to chat to him and to try and engage him in a 'conversation'. I was very struck that this baby still wasn't able to engage like this, and that there was no sound or movement happening while he was lying on his back. We'd expect a baby of this age to be making lots of noises, sustaining a good 'conversation' and for their arms and legs to be moving all the time as a very active part of the interaction. When I asked the foster carer to turn Dale onto his tummy, we could see that he wasn't able to hold his head up or support his weight on his arms.

I talked to the foster carers more about this, wondering how they were finding things at home. They felt terribly concerned about him – he was having three hours of contact five days a week with his birth parents and was very distressed during and after those contacts, often crying for hours, and they were finding him hard to soothe at these times. They talked about a week where there had been no contact and that being the only time that they'd seen the beginnings of Dale feeling settled and starting to make a connection with them.

So from this, I hope you begin to get an idea that it takes a lot more than removing a baby from a harmful situation for their experiences to be classed as 'good enough'. Dale was spending too much time in a stressed and anxious state of mind, and this in turn was getting in the way of him being able to develop on a bodily or emotional level. He could not be said to be thriving in the current circumstances and it was important to talk to the social worker about my observations and concerns. I was really pleased that these were helpful (in part in reinforcing the concerns of other professionals who could see that things weren't right) and that significant changes were made very quickly.

We'll keep returning to these early stages of development as we think about the patterns of movement in children and young people who haven't been in the kinds of environments that have allowed their bodies to follow this pattern of development. I'd really encourage you to spend as much time as you can observing babies in different settings – in their home and in childcare settings. Try and notice the way that all of this moving happens within a relational context in those early days.

Chapter 4

A BUSS Assessment

MEETING children and families as part of an assessment process is complex. I'm going to assume that the basic principles of working with families are already familiar to practitioners. Any assessment is, of course, only the start of the process and it's just the same here. The BUSS model typically runs as a four-stage intervention, taking place over a three-month period. It starts with a training day for parents, carers, fostering/adoption social workers and support staff and schools. This is followed, about a week later, by an assessment session with a child and their parents or carers. Session 3 is run as a group for parents or carers four weeks after the initial assessment, and Session 4 is a reassessment of the child along with their parents or carers, four weeks after that. Families (and schools, if they have attended the training day and indicated a willingness to be involved) are sent a summary of the assessment and each of the subsequent sessions, with ideas of games and activities for the child.

Measuring change

As with most interventions, it's helpful to establish a baseline of where you're starting so that you can set appropriate goals and accurately measure change. Research around the efficacy of this model is in its early stages and, at the time of writing, there are a number of projects at various stages of completion. Early indicators are that the outcomes of the research are in line with the clinical observations and feedback over the last six years from therapists, parents, carers, schools and, most importantly, the children and young people themselves, which has been very positive.

This model focuses on developing movement within the context of a nurturing relationship. When looking for evidence of change, I expect to see change in bodily and emotional regulation, as well as the parent–child relationship. Accredited practitioners use the BUSS screening tool that I've developed and we generally use this alongside a questionnaire that measures parent–child relations. I particularly like Kim Golding's 'Thinking about your child' questionnaire, which is available on the developmental dyadic psychotherapy website.[1] This combination allows us to capture changes in bodily regulation and emotional regulation relationships.

Some more ideas for noticing movement

It can be hard to know how to decide whether an intervention like BUSS might be helpful. We thought about noticing movement in Chapter 2, and I'd like to think a bit more about that here. We can't see sensory integration happening, just as we can't see the workings of our computer but, in the same way that we can get clues about the working of the computer from what's happening on the screen, we can observe children moving and notice patterns of movement and behaviour. It's important not to attribute huge significance to an isolated event; one thing on its own might not be significant, but when it clusters together with a few other things from the same system, it becomes more compelling to try and understand what's happening.

It's generally easiest to observe children and young people as they move around doing everyday activities like walking, going up and down a flight of stairs, running, writing or using cutlery. An environment like the post-adoption Stay and Play events are a perfect opportunity for a bit of unobtrusive observation of how children are moving, without making them self-conscious about being watched!

I find that children learn ways to compensate and use other parts of their bodies to make up for the parts that don't work as well, so it's important to look at *how* they're tackling an activity, not just what they're doing. It's helpful to observe children in a setting that's familiar

---

1   https://ddpnetwork.org/library/thinking-child

to the child, perhaps when they're playing outside or at a playground with peers (without developmental trauma) and notice how they're holding themselves, moving about and tackling the apparatus. A child might be able to climb up onto the climbing frame, but just how they do that is what's going to give good information about their foundation systems. You can also get good information from noticing everyday things at home, like how they sit at the table and eat their meals or carry a glass of juice. Notice whether when they sit to watch TV, they're sitting in a relaxed way or constantly moving and changing position. It's also helpful to notice what the quality of the movement is like. Do they move in a fluid, well-coordinated way? Does their body work in a well-synchronized way so that they're able to do what they want to do without bumping into things or tripping over? Is there smoothness about the movement?

It is also useful to think about whether their body is giving good, reliable signals about things like whether they're hungry, when they're full, if they can taste what they're eating and enjoy a range of different tastes and textures. Other clues can come from thinking about what sort of state of mind they're in most of the time. Are they able to stay in the moment of an experience and enjoy what's happening or do they struggle to cope when they don't know something; do they seem quite comfortable in themselves or do they seem vigilant and stressed, as if they're expecting something bad to happen?

SEAN: EARLY DAYS AT GYM CLUB

Watching Sean (who was six) climb up onto a mat at the BUSS gym club that I run in Leeds was a good example of this idea of it not being what a child does, but how they do it. The mats are quite big, and about as high as Sean's ribs. When we watch the children in the preschool class climb onto these same mats, they face the mat, stretch their arms out onto the mat and then do a move that involves a combination of jumping, climbing, pushing with their legs and pulling with their arms. When we first met, Sean would climb up onto the mats by turning himself around so that his back was against the mat, then jump as high as he could, throwing himself back at the same time, so that he landed with his back on the mat. This might take a few tries. He then used his legs to flip his body over onto his tummy and then his legs again to push his body up into standing. Knowing that he was doing this because his system was underdeveloped rather than being broken, we encouraged Sean to try and stay facing the mat and teach his arms and shoulders how to pull him up onto it – so much better! Imagine how it would feel to go through life having to use your legs to power and stabilize all your moves and your arms not being an integral part of your body and movement – it amazes me that these children manage as well as they do in everyday life!

It can be helpful to make recordings of a child moving around and playing – it's often easier to try and work out what's happening when you've got the chance to replay it a few times! I ask families I'm working with to make lots of recordings of things as they go along, and it can be great to sit with the whole family and look back on their progress and how far they've come.

Children with developmental trauma won't necessarily stand out from their peers at first glance, but as you learn and notice how children are doing things, and about the foundation systems, I hope that you'll get a new lens to look through and make sense of what you're seeing.

Thinking with parents about their observations of how their child moves

If children are able to manage all of the things like sitting to eat, running, going up and down a flight of stairs, hopping, skipping and riding a bike without any difficulty, or are, for example, really good gymnasts, then they probably don't need an intervention like this. But if parents and carers notice some gaps in their child's systems – perhaps they've got no difficulties with some of the areas but struggle with others – then it's worth pursuing. It's rare to see a child whose systems are universally underdeveloped; it's much more common to meet children who've got islands of good functioning and then other parts of the system that aren't as well developed as they need them to be.

Being prepared

By this I'm talking about both the families and the workers! Starting with families, I begin any intervention by making sure that parents have a good understanding of the principles of the BUSS model. I have nearly always worked with the parents and school on a training day, where I have outlined the model and reinforced the idea of systems being underdeveloped and needing to be rebuilt through relationships with known and trusted adults.

INTRODUCTION TO THE BUSS MODEL

We usually spend some time within the training playing some of the games so that parents, teachers and support workers have had the chance to experience them for themselves and get a sense of how it feels for them. We talk through norms of development and think about what they've noticed about how their child moves and how tuned in to themselves they seem on a bodily level. We spend a lot of time separating out emotional regulation from bodily regulation and I try to emphasize the importance of following the blueprint of typical development – trying to get bodily regulation before building complex social or emotional skills. My first book, *Improving Sensory Processing in Traumatised Children* (Lloyd 2016), is a useful introduction for parents and carers as they think about this model.

All of this preparatory work makes it much easier to work in a collaborative way with parents and schools; it is not rare and exclusive knowledge. I constantly reinforce my belief that parents are the experts on their children: I can join them and bring a BUSS lens and way of looking at things, but I want to add this to their expertise, and for them to know that they are the crux of where we go after the assessment. It is their relationship, knowledge of their child and work that are going to allow the child to grow into themselves on a bodily level.

The room

This is so important and, generally, if I'm not seeing a child in their own home (which is a good place to do the assessment because you get a great picture of the sorts of activities that are going to be possible in the space available), then I try to use a room that is spacious but fairly dull. I find that if I'm in a room in somewhere like a children's centre, where there are all sorts of interesting toys, it's almost impossible to persuade the child that the thing I'm asking them to do (like commando crawling when they can barely manage lying on their tummies) is more interesting than playing with the toys that are all around! It's then much more difficult to tell whether the child isn't engaging because the activity is really challenging and their foundation systems are underdeveloped, or if they are just much keener on playing with the toys in the room.

Noticing more than movement

As with any assessment, it is important to notice all of the 'relationship music' that's playing in the background when you're asking children and families to play the different games and activities. We can learn so much from noticing the extent to which the child is able to accept, or the parent is able to offer, help and support. There's a very different feel to the sessions where the parent is really struggling and it feels as if they need the child to be at their worst, and those sessions where parents are trying to support their child to be the best they can be. All of this is important: if a parent really is at the end of their tether, then the chances are they're not going to have the emotional or practical energy to do the kinds of games and activities you have in mind. Remember the table for the jigsaw in Chapter 2 – it's only after making sure parents or carers have got enough support for themselves that it's useful to introduce this model. Otherwise, it's better to wait until there's likely to be a bit of spare capacity.

There are other times when it's helpful for the intervention to be more heavily supported, perhaps by adoption support workers or other therapists who are interested in using this model and who have at least Level 2 BUSS training (see Introduction). For example, if I notice lots of what seem like quite small remarks a parent might make, such as, 'She'll never do that for me' when I'm carrying out the assessment, then I'll take that quite seriously and think about what help the parents might need to get them to a place when they feel they can support their child to do the things we're needing them to do.

Preparing children for a BUSS assessment

It's important to let a child know what we're going to do and why they're here. I try and keep this very simple but say that I'm someone who works with children and sometimes I meet children whose bodies work really well and are really good at doing what they want them to do, and other times I meet children who find that harder. I explain that we're here today to see if there's anything we can do to get their body working even better for them. Sometimes, with older children, I might talk briefly about early environments and babies missing out on the kind of loving and movement experiences they need to have to get their body functioning as well as it can, but I really tend to be guided by the parents and take my lead from them. I do usually ask children if they've thought about this at all and am often surprised by how in tune with themselves they are. I met a little boy (aged eight at the time) who said that he thought his arms worked quite well and his legs worked quite well, but they didn't seem to work well together, which turned out to be a very accurate description! For other children, it's only when we really start to improve their bodily awareness and functioning that they might be able to look back and reflect on how it was before. But generally, once a child has moved on to the next stage, they're more concerned with looking forward than looking back.

Preparing parents for the assessment

When I'm doing an assessment, I don't usually tell children if they're getting things right or wrong (unless they can see) but try to be very positive and encouraging. I want them to leave the assessment keen to play the games again and having a sense that they're good at them. It's helpful to prime the parents about this before the assessment. The purpose of the assessment is twofold: to establish a starting point to rebuild the foundation systems and to enthuse the child with the idea that doing these games and activities every day at home is going to be fun and worthwhile. If the child leaves the assessment feeling as if they've failed, then I haven't done my job and I've made the parent's job much harder. I find if parents can understand this before we start, they are much less likely to point out any mistakes the child is making, and are also more likely to be aware that they need to be noticing what's happening because they might not get any clues from what I'm saying to the child.

Materials

This will make more sense when we start to think about the assessment, but it might be helpful to provide a summary of the basic things I use:

- Table and chairs of the right height for the child you're seeing. We want the child to sit at the table and for their hips, knees and feet to be at an angle of 90 degrees with their feet flat on the floor. I realize this sounds a bit pedantic, but I'd be drummed out of the occupational therapy profession if I didn't talk about seating! It's especially important because I will notice how the child sits and make assumptions about their foundation systems from this. However, if a child is sitting on a chair that's too big for them and their feet can't touch the ground, there's no way of knowing whether their legs are swinging because they can't touch the floor, or because they are needing to move around a lot to get a sense of their body and where they are. If it's completely impossible to have a child-sized table and chairs when I'm doing the assessment (for example, if I'm in someone's house and they only have regular furniture), then I try and have a box with me that the child can put their feet on so that when they're sitting on adult-sized chairs at an adult-sized table then at least their feet are on a stable surface and their hips and knees can be at 90 degrees.

- Somewhere comfortable for parents to sit beside the child.

- It's also really helpful if there are sofas in the room that it's okay for children to put their feet on.

- Feely bag (I'll talk about content later).

- Some kind of small, roller massage ball.

- Two climbing ropes, about 1 metre long each.

- Crisps of a variety of flavours.

- Straws of different sizes.

- Twelve cushions, all the same size.

- Unlined paper and pencil.

- Soft blanket (this is to put on the floor to crawl on).

Chapter 5

The Tactile System

T HE tactile system is made up of millions of receptors all over our body, in our skin and in our mouths. These receptors are on the surface and in deeper layers of our skin, and register and respond to touch and sensation, carrying the information from the skin to the central nervous system. Touch is often described as the first language of the human baby – highly developed a long time before we have speech. Touch allows us to make a physical connection, to nurture, soothe and calm a baby, while at the same time, touch and vision allow the baby to explore their environment and begin to put all of this information together to form a picture of their surroundings.

The tactile system is an evolving system; at the beginning of the baby's life it is set up as a defensive system, alert to danger and anything that might harm the baby. In common with all of our sensory systems, the evolution of the system is largely unconscious and entirely dependent on the experience of the child. Within a  safe, loving, nurturing environment, the system shifts over the first months and years of life from a system that is all about survival to one that allows us to explore and experience our environment. Without those experiences of being well cared for and nurtured, the system doesn't develop beyond its defensive functioning – which really makes a lot of sense. If the baby can't feel confident that someone else can be responsible for their survival, they need to hold on to everything within their power to try and ensure their own survival. If we think about the loving care that the baby needs in the first year, feeding, holding and touch are a huge part of this, and these form the building blocks to relationships. The baby gets to know themselves on a bodily level through the relationship that is provided by the parent – as well as getting to know the people in their family. Winnicott (1957) talked about there being no such thing as a baby and mother, just a nursing couple. Without the predictable, loving care of a known and trusted adult, the baby is destined to stay in this defensive state of mind – everything is primed for survival.

Our tactile receptors respond to different kinds of sensory input, for example touch, taste and smell. These messages are then carried to the brain and central nervous system and used to inform our actions or understanding of our environment. The whole system is fascinating, and different receptors have different 'tasks'. For example, there are five different receptors for touch, each with a specialist function; one set of receptors has the job of discerning and responding to pressure, another set fires rapidly when an object first touches our palm. The messages travel at different speeds, according to their role and function. The touch receptors that detect pain travel very quickly so as to alert us to danger and allow us to take action to protect ourselves. You've probably noticed this yourself if you've burned your hand – sometimes you've pulled your hand away from the heat source before you've even registered, at a cognitive level, what's happening.

It's a fantastically sophisticated and complex system, responsible for a huge range of actions, from protection and safety to minutely precise information that allows us to do complex and intricate tasks. Different parts of our bodies are much more responsive to touch than others. You probably remember playing those kind of lap games with small children, where you use your finger to play games on the palm of their hand – I remember 'Round and round the garden' – but if you were to do the same action on, for example, the outside of your forearm, you'd find it much less discerning of the touch because of the distribution of the different receptors.

The tactile system is closely linked to the visual system – think of how touching and feeling an object allows us to build our visual picture of it. On a neurological level, the tactile system is closely intertwined with the proprioceptive system (which receives and make sense of information from inside the body) and if you read traditional sensory integration books (and remember these are aimed at people with a sensory processing disorder, not an underdeveloped system) then these two systems are often brought together and termed the 'somatosensory' system. The BUSS model separates the two systems because understanding the evolution of the tactile system gives us a great way of helping to recalibrate the limbic system for children who are operating in a really heightened state of arousal a lot of the time.

Just thinking for a moment about this evolution from a system primed for survival in the early days and weeks to one that has shifted to exploration, I remember when one of my children was a tiny baby and we were in the bath together. She was only about six weeks old and we were having a lovely time – I was singing quietly to her, the water was warm, it was all good. But then she turned her face to take a mouthful of the warm liquid and then, realizing it wasn't delicious breast milk, she screamed. Not just a small expression of distaste, but distress, outrage and disgust, so noisy that her daddy came running in to see what on earth was wrong. At that stage of her development, her whole system was primed for survival – is this going to aid my survival? If not, it's a threat and must be responded to as such.

If we fast forward a couple of years – again the same child is in the bath, this time with her sister, and now, what's more fun than to take a mouthful of bathwater and spurt it at your sister/parent/ the wall? This time, great hilarity ensues, and it's repeated many times! The infant's tactile system that was primed for survival has evolved into one that can play, explore and have fun. The physiological evolution of the tactile system from this defensive to discriminatory function is exactly what makes it so helpful for us when we're trying to support children whose actions and reactions are about survival rather than being able to absorb the good things that are available to them in their current environment.

Feeding

The tactile system is concerned with making sense of all tactile stimuli from outside the body, as well as touch. It's helpful, within this system, to think about early feeding experiences and how important they are in the development of the tactile system. If we try and picture what a good experience of feeding might look like, we'll see a parent or carer in a calm, available state, in a place that's not too hot, cold or noisy and we'll see them tuned in to the baby who is also in a calm and settled state. The parent or carer is able to respond to the signals the baby gives out, noticing things like whether the baby is drinking too quickly or is not able to latch on well enough, and making adjustments, perhaps changing the baby's position or giving them a break, and then continuing with the feed until the baby feels themselves to be full, stops feeding, and is in that wonderful satiated state of well-being. But there are so many things that can get in the way of this, from the parent or carer's state of mind, to other demands and distractions, to the baby's state of mind or how developed the baby is on a physiological basis.

Unfortunately for many babies who are in families struggling to meet their needs, feeding is fraught, irregular and a long way away from the attuned, paced experience that we'd really like it to be. Even for children in foster care, the demands of contact schedules or appointments mean that it's rarely possible for feeding to happen at the infant's pace and timing. In fact, I've rarely met a looked-after child whose early feeding experiences were as good as we might want them to be, which is why I think that this is such a good opportunity to go back and lay down different experiences alongside those earlier traumatic ones. I'm aiming to do lots of things within this; for some children, it's slowing the whole process down so that they're actually tasting what they're eating rather than just eating as if they don't know when their next meal is going to be; for other children, it's trying to increase oral strength so that they can chew better – or so the articulation of their words becomes more distinct – or so that they don't dribble so much; for others, it's helping to build good associations between what I call 'mouthly' activities and fun; the list could go on and on. But there's always the relationship at the heart of it – rebuilding these underdeveloped bodily systems within a nurturing relationship – and when we're thinking of the tactile system, that's such an important part. It's not just about going through the motions of some activities to rebuild function, it's about function growing through the relationship, in the same way that feeding isn't just about getting nutrition into the baby.

In that early feeding experience, there are so many opportunities for baby and mother to really get to know each other – from the positioning of feeding that allows for lots of body contact between mother and baby, to the mutual gaze. Even newborns can see the distance from the breast to the mother's face and they can watch each other as the baby feeds – we want that baby to be drinking in love and care along with the milk. The mother can tune in to the minutiae of the baby – the way they move as they feed, the noises they make, the stages of the feed – it's got so much potential to be such an enriching experience when it goes well. It's easy to idealize that early infant–parent experience, and it's rarely that simple, but it's good to know the potential and possibilities so that as we deviate from that, for whatever reason, we can be aware of what's missing and make efforts to fill in those gaps.

Let's think for a moment about the basic physiology of the newborn baby feeding. It's a fascinating action – highly effective when it works well and yet really fragile. Frick and colleagues (1996) have written a really useful little leaflet for parents about the mechanics of feeding. They talk about the suck, swallow, breath synchrony in a way that I find really helpful when I'm working with children whose oral systems are underdeveloped. For typically developing babies, this suck, swallow, breath synchrony develops around 37 weeks in utero, by which time the baby is drinking about a litre of amniotic fluid a day. This means that by the time the baby is born at around 40 weeks, the building blocks needed for feeding are already in place.

Frick describes the stages of the synchrony, starting with suck. To suck, the baby has to be able to form a seal using their top lip and their tongue. This seal allows the baby to suck the milk into their mouth. The tongue forms itself into a container for the milk (by making a groove, the sides of which are formed by the tongue pressing against the top of the mouth). As this container fills up, the milk reaches the back of the mouth, and the sensation of the milk at the back of the mouth triggers a swallow. We can't breathe and swallow at the same time and so breathing is halted to allow for swallowing and, once the milk has been swallowed, breathing can start again and the whole process continues, like a series of waves going into the shore.

This system is so dependent on that interplay of relationship and physiology that I'm always surprised if this part of the system is as well developed as it can be when there have been tensions or trauma in a child's early experiences. For me, it's really helpful to think and talk carefully to parents and carers about their child's relationship with food and also to observe oral functioning in all its forms – talking, eating, drinking and whether the child is putting lots of things up to or into their mouth or dribbling a lot more than you'd expect.

JANEY, LEROY AND LENNY: BUILDING ORAL STRENGTH

JANEY

Sometimes, this is quite easy to notice and I find that it's possible to rebuild this part of the system fairly quickly, as was the case with Janey, who was four years old when I met her and her parents. She'd recently been adopted and, while she was a delightful and engaging little girl, it was very difficult to understand what she was saying and she was constantly dribbling. I met her just before the summer holidays and she was due to start school in the September. I shared her parents' concerns about her starting school when her speech was so hard to understand that she wouldn't even be able to tell other children what she was called. We talked about how much this would get in the way of her being able to make friends as well as learning. We agreed that, given there was no time to get a speech and language assessment or intervention completed before she started school, we'd start by thinking of it as an underdeveloped tactile system, knowing that Janey's early nurture and feeding experiences had been woefully inadequate. I suggested different ideas for games that involved blowing, sucking, taste and touch (explanations of these are given in Chapter 8) and the family were fantastic at building these into their everyday routine so that they were able to do them lots of times a day. When I met with Janey and her parents again four weeks later, I was delighted to have her tell me, really clearly, that her name was Janey, and to see that she was no longer dribbling. A great result for her family for a month of intensive work!

LEROY

Another example of underdeveloped oral strength is Leroy, who we met in Chapter 2, where I described him sitting down in his chair to eat his lunch, which, I didn't mention at the time, was a delicious-looking egg sandwich. To eat this, he lifted the top slice of bread off the sandwich and then scraped the filling across his bottom teeth so that it landed in his mouth, then he swallowed. He didn't eat the bread at all and his foster carer said that he didn't like anything that involved chewing.

Just as we'd done with Janey, once his foster carer understood the idea of his system being underdeveloped because of his early experiences, she too was able to play lots of blowing and sucking games with him to develop oral strength and stamina.

LENNY

There are other times when the underdeveloped tactile system is just one part of the picture, as was the case with Lenny. Lenny was five years old when I first met him. I was in his class as part of my CAMHS work, doing an ADHD assessment on another child, but Lenny caught my eye because of the speed at which he was doing everything – he was like a little rocket, zooming round the classroom, knocking into other children, bumping into tables. It wasn't long after this that I met his adoptive mum and it was good to be able to make some sense of what I'd seen! We'll think about the whizzing and bumping when we look at vestibular and proprioceptive systems, but while we're thinking about tactile systems, it's worth noticing a couple of things. The first was his mum's description of how much Lenny chewed when he was feeling anxious. He'd chewed the sleeves off eight school coats in the term I met them – literally chewed them right off up to about the elbow. The second was that he never seemed to be still – his mum never really felt that she had his attention or that he was fully with her. She understood this in terms of hypervigilance, with Lenny constantly being in a state of high alert. His mum knew that, on a physiological level, Lenny would have spent much of his early life in this fight or flight state, but she was keen to try and help shore up his sense of safety and well-being now that things were very different. It was useful to be able to apply the principles of underdeveloped systems to both these aspects of Lenny's presentation.

It's always distressing to see children whose early experiences have left them wary and fearful of everyone and everything; it's as if that part of their system is stuck in time. By the time I meet them, they're usually in families who behave very differently, where there are sensitive, attuned caregivers, with lots of opportunities for nurture and growth, and yet so often they continue to respond to situations in that same defensive way, as if they're still in their original situation. Changing the external environment hasn't changed their internal one and this is where we need to start – recalibrating the limbic system from its state of high alert that means it rushes straight to the fight/flight/freeze response to one that is able to tune in to the moment of the experience and discern what's happening. To do this, we need first to know what state of mind the child is in and the extent to which they're able to stay in the moment of an experience and manage the uncertainty of not knowing.

The BUSS model uses games that mimic the physiological development of the tactile system to help decrease defensive functioning on a psychological as well as a bodily level.

We know that children develop bodily regulation through those early nurturing relationships, so when we're thinking about children who may be older in age but not well regulated on a bodily level, we need first to develop that relationship so that it can be our vehicle for development. There's a parallel process here too – as children become more regulated on a bodily level, their capacity to relate grows. So we start by developing relationships with known and trusted adults using the kinds of games and sensory experiences that allow the primitive tactile system to evolve and, by doing this, we can begin to recalibrate the limbic system from its state of high alert to the child being able to stay in the moment of an experience and for things to grow from there.

There are so many games and activities that can be useful here. I usually give families some ideas to get started and then it's great when families build on them and develop their own games. It's getting that starting point right that is so important because the challenge for that individual child's system within that particular family must be at the right level – too hard and the child (and family) will disengage (and risk compounding that sense of failure and never getting things right); too easy and it's not going to extend their level of functioning.

LENNY: RE-FEEDING A HUNGRY TACTILE SYSTEM

If we apply this to Lenny, thinking in terms of tactile functioning and a system that should, by Lenny's age, have moved from defensive to discriminatory functioning, allowing Lenny to stay in the moment of an experience and be able to absorb information and experiences, we can see how underdeveloped it was. I'll talk more about exactly what we did in the next couple of chapters, but by treating the chewing and the constantly flitting from one thing to another using games and activities that mimicked the ways the tactile system should develop, we were able to bring Lenny's system up to a level so that it wasn't constantly needing to be 'fed' by chewing things or to be so on the lookout for danger in situations where he wasn't needing to be. I often talk with parents and carers about the idea of these systems being 'hungry' and that we need to feed them with the experiences they didn't have when they should have had them.

Chapter 6

Assessing the Development of the Tactile System

I DIVIDE this stage of the assessment into three parts, each one looking at the different functions of the tactile system. They all also give lots of opportunities to notice the extent to which the child is able to manage not being in charge of what's happening, and the uncertainty of not knowing exactly what's going to happen. It's very important to gather this information alongside the more 'hands-on' material.

- Part 1 looks at discriminatory tactile function and trying to see whether the child is getting the information they need about what they are touching and feeling from their hands.

- Part 2 looks at how the child responds to being touched: whether they're over or under responding.

- Part 3 looks at oral functioning – again, thinking about that spectrum of defensive to discriminatory functioning as well as looking at oral strength and stamina. This is the part of the assessment where we can begin to see how the child is registering messages about sensations from inside their body.

The materials I use for this part of the assessment are the feely bag, a roller ball, bowls that are big enough to hold some crisps, chocolate buttons or grapes, and some straws.

I usually start my assessments with these activities – partly because we sit at a table to do them and the child can stay sitting on or with their parents if they want to, or they can come and sit with me at the small table and chairs I use (right beside their parents).

It's a good way to begin to get to know the child. I often spend a few minutes chatting before we start and that seems to work well to help the child sense that it's going to be okay being here and what we're going to do is fun – but for other children, it can be best just to get started. With all three foundation systems I'll outline the assessment and then think about ways I grade it if it's either too easy or too challenging for the child.

This part of the assessment also gives much more information about the child and the parent–child relationship. It's important to notice how the child approaches the tasks, as well as how they perform. I always try and look for signs of how anxious or uncertain the child is feeling: are they too anxious to even come into the room or sit down? Do they immediately say, 'I'm not doing this' or 'That's too hard' before I've finished explaining what we are going to be doing? Or do they try and take control, deciding that we'll play the game that's inside their head rather than mine? It's also good to notice the extent to which a child is able to turn to their parents or carers for help and support, as well as the way that support is offered.

Part 1: Building up a picture of discriminatory tactile functioning – the child doing the touching
Feely bag game

Feely bags are a great, simple way to get started (and that's important as I don't want to overwhelm parents with fancy gadgets or therapy aids – I want to reinforce the idea that they can do at home everything that we do as part of the assessment today). This is a typical feely bag for me.

As you can see, there is a range of objects that are familiar but distinct from each other. The number of objects might depend on the age of the child – I'd have fewer things (perhaps six) for a younger child and maybe as many as 12 with an older child. And again, working on the principle of starting from a point of success and building from there,

I often keep a few more objects to one side so that I can add them in, making it harder and at the same time making sure the child knows that they must be doing really well because we need the extra ones. It's important to have objects that feel quite different from each other to start with – I want to build on success, so having things like a fork and a small soft toy means that most children can start off by getting things right. And if a child really struggles to discern the things as different and distinct to begin with, then you have a good idea of just how different you now need to make things.

As you'll see when we come to think about grading this activity, it's helpful to have a couple of duplicates in the bag – for example, two batteries or two stones – as well as objects that are different in size, like a piece of duplo and a key.

First, I put the bag on the table and tell the child that I've got lots of different things in there and that we're going to play a game with them. I ask the child (and their parents or carers) to see if they can guess what might be in the bag by feeling from the outside. When they've had a bit of a feel and a guess about what might be in there, I suggest that we tip the bag out and together we look at and feel all the objects. It's important to establish a common language for the things in the bag at this stage; for example, I have a golf ball in my feely bag as well as a marble that is about the same size. I need to know that the child understands which ball I'm asking them to find so that I can know whether they're getting it right or not. I don't need them to know that one is called a golf ball and one is a marble, I just need to be sure that they can tell the difference between a ball that's bumpy on the outside and a smooth ball.

Once I'm sure the child has touched and felt all of the objects, I put them back in the bag and explain that we're going to play a game called, 'No Eyes' (hamming it up with your voice at this point generally makes it sound a bit more exciting!), and I'm going to ask them to put their hand into the bag and find the object that I ask them to – but without using their eyes. I always start with bigger, easier objects (like the Duplo® or a fork) then make it progressively harder as the child is able to succeed. It can make it more fun to involve parents too – I often ask children if they'd like to see if mum or dad can do this (having primed mum and dad first not to make it look too easy!) and ask them if they think their parents would like to try easy, hard or super hard. All of this gives great information about the child's sense of themselves and their own confidence, as well as lots of opportunities to notice parent–child interactions. It's interesting to see which hand a child chooses to put in, but I generally suggest that, to start with, they use the hand they use to write with at school.

After the child has succeeded with the first couple of objects (or if they can't find them, I make it a very short game) then I want to make it incrementally harder, so will ask the child to find something that is a bit smaller or a bit less distinct – like one of the bracelets or a battery. Some children find things very quickly and easily while for others it's clearly very tricky. It's important to just go at the speed of the child – if a child is taking a long time to find things, I'll try and be encouraging, noticing how carefully their hands are looking and helping them to keep trying until they can find it. As with any assessment, noticing the process as well as the outcome is important. So if a child just can't wait or can't manage to find anything without looking, I'll just notice that, and maybe say something like, 'Those eyes are really wanting to help your hands'. With some children it might be appropriate to wonder if they might be able to let those hands try on their own, but for others it's about noticing that and then seeing how that progresses with practice over the weeks ahead.

I'd like to introduce another couple of children here: Elsa and Sean, both of whom were six and in Year 1 at school when I met them. Elsa was very quiet and reserved when I first met her, hiding behind her parents, while Sean burst into the room and was already going at top speed. We'll think about them throughout the book, starting with this first part of the tactile system.

ELSA AND SEAN: PART 1 – USING THE FEELY BAG TO ASSESS DISCRIMINATION

ELSA

Elsa was really fast and accurate with this game, not using her eyes at all and picking up and holding the different objects as she looked for the one she was wanting to find. It was clear that her confidence in herself wasn't high so we progressed through her finding the golf ball, the marble, the car, the bracelet, the fork, the pencil and the stone, first with her dominant and then with her non-dominant hand, until she agreed she'd like to make it harder. I then asked her to use both hands in the bag at the same time and to find the same thing with each hand – first the batteries and then the bracelets. Again, she was able to do this easily, and it was beginning to look as if she thought she might be able to manage the assessment. It was also lovely to see the gentle encouragement and praise her parents were giving her throughout this.

SEAN

Sean approached the game quite differently – he'd said, 'This is so easy for me' before we'd even started. He struggled to wait until I'd finished the explanation before he was wanting to get started, and his movements were all very 'crashy' and 'bangy' as he picked up the bag and tried to find the things. He wasn't able to find them instantly and kept having quick peeks into the bag to see where the object was. I didn't progress past finding the car, marble and fork, because I already had enough information. We needed to work on both parts of this system – staying in the moment of the experience, and the discriminatory functioning.

Part 2: Building up a picture of discriminatory tactile functioning – the child being touched
Roller ball on the palm of the child's hand

To do this I've got a small massage ball that looks like a plant pot but that opens up to be a small roller ball called a flower pot massage ball. It doesn't have to be a roller ball like this, but it's useful and they're easily sourced on eBay. I usually start by demonstrating on a parent and explaining to the child that I'm going to ask them to put their hand on the table, palm up, with their fingers as wide apart as they can get them. I say that I'm going to roll the ball around their palm and up one of their fingers. Then I'm going to ask them to close their eyes and see if they can guess which finger I rolled up with the ball. We usually do a bit of practice of this where the child has their eyes open – I just want to make it feel familiar and non-threatening. I tend to repeat this a few time with both hands, asking and noticing how it feels for the child. If a child is a bit hesitant, I get them to do it on their parents (and themselves) for a while until they are happy for either their parent or me to do it. It really doesn't matter which of us does it, the important things are to just notice how it feels and how the child manages.

Sometimes children don't much like closing their eyes and they might prefer to just look away. That's fine, and again I just notice this and when I meet them again am curious about whether it still feels like that.

It's important to do this the same each time, so I roll the ball around their hand a couple of times, then up and down the finger a couple of times, giving quite a lot of sensory input but not pressing down hard. I ask the child to use their other hand to point to the finger I rolled the ball up.

It's good to try this on yourself. Generally, most people can tell which finger is being touched – the palm of your hand is a very sensitive part of your body and so if a child really can't feel anything at all, then we know that we need to play lots of games to help with this.

It's helpful to do it with both hands. I often find that when children are very reliant on a dominant hand, the other is quite neglected. I sometimes see this in older children, just by the way they're sitting and holding themselves, where their non-dominant hand is almost a bit behind them. It's not unusual for a child to be able to feel what's happening on their dominant hand but not on their non-dominant, and again this is good information about where to begin.

If a child isn't able to discern this, I don't go any further. If they are, I ask them if we can make it a bit harder and progress to drawing on their back with the ball. (I often have to explain that when I say 'drawing on your back' to a child, I do not mean drawing with a pen – I've had some horrified looks from children who thought we were going to get into so much trouble for drawing on their clothes!)

ELSA AND SEAN: PART 2 – RESPONDING TO TOUCH

Elsa and Sean were both really good at this part of the assessment, and by this I mean they were registering being touched accurately and were neither over-responsive (becoming squirmy and wriggling) nor under-responsive (not noticing what was happening) to the touch. I was conscious of doing this quickly with Sean, wanting to get an idea about how under- or over-responsive he was to touch, but before he lost interest or moved on to something else.

KEEPING THE OTHER SYSTEMS IN MIND

I don't want to confuse things by veering into proprioceptive functioning, but the feely bag game and the rolling the ball on the palm of the hand game also give useful information about whether a child is holding and handling the objects with their whole hand or doing much more fingertip touching, and whether that early palmar grasp reflex is still around. Thinking back to Chapter 3 on the sequential nature of development, we know that for typically developing children crawling is very important in the development of the arches of the hand that allow our hands to mould around the objects that we're touching, and to have good flat hands with fingers facing forwards (not curling in). I aim just to notice that at this stage and ask parents about it – but I'll work on this area using games and activities to develop the proprioceptive and vestibular systems.

As I'll discuss more when we think about Rory, it's always important to be mindful of a child's previous experience of touch and to have thought with parents and carers about how the child might manage this part of the assessment. I always make sure that we establish safe boundaries at the beginning of this part of the assessment, so that the child feels comfortable and in control of what's happening.

Simple figure on back

I use the roller ball for this and explain to the child that I'm going to 'draw' shapes or letters on their back and see if they can guess what I'm doing. Again, if they're a bit unsure of this, I let them try it on their parent's back, or ask their parent to do the drawing rather than me doing it. To start, I rub the child's back with my flat palm in a downward direction, from their neck to their waist, just to 'clear' it. Then, if the child is of an age to know what the letter that's at the beginning of their name looks like, I draw that big, capital letter on their back. If they don't know their letters, I do a straight-sided shape. I then rub their back clean again with that same downward stroke and this time do a different kind of letter or shape – so if the first letter of their name has been a straight-sided letter, like an A or an M, then I do a curvy letter, like an S, or vice versa.

I then rub that letter/shape off and tell the child that I'm going to make it harder now – I'm either going to draw an A/straight-sided shape or I'm going to draw an S/wavy-sided shape and see if they can guess which one I've drawn. I usually do this four or five times until I'm clear about whether the child is getting it right from lucky guesses or if they do seem to be able to discern what I'm doing. Rubbing or 'cleaning' the child's back between guesses, using firmer pressure down the child's back with flat, still hands, is generally settling to the system and gives a good restarting point each time.

If the child can do this, then we can make it harder again, as I did with Elsa.

ELSA AND SEAN: PART 2 – RESPONDING TO TOUCH, LOOKING AT DISCRIMINATION

ELSA

Elsa flew through this game. She sat very still while I rolled the ball on her back, and really enjoyed being able to guess each of the letters correctly. Because she was so good at it and enjoying it and I wanted to build her confidence for the vestibular and proprioceptive parts of the assessment (I could see from the way that she'd walked up the stairs and how she was sitting that these were going to be much more challenging to her), we expanded it a bit to be either an E for Elsa, an M for mum, a D for dad or an S for Sarah. We then did the same thing again with non-capital letters – and she got them all right too!

SEAN

Sean found this one much trickier. He was really squirmy and wriggly as soon as I started to roll the ball on his back – very over-responsive to the touch. To try and settle his system down a bit I got him to lie on his tummy over his mum's knee and she did the letters on his back, with lots of the firm, flat, still hand 'cleaning' of his back between each letter. This really helped him to be less squirmy but he still struggled to discern the different letters. I wasn't sure whether part of this might be about him not being very confident with his letters and so we tried with shapes as well, but it was a similar picture.

Cat on back

If a child can accurately discern the letters or shapes on their back, the last step is to draw a more complicated picture on their back, and I use a cat. I usually draw it out for the child first on paper so they can see it – head, big fat body, wiggly tail, ears and whiskers. It doesn't have to be a cat, just something that's recognizable to the child and has five distinct elements that are different from each other. I then draw it on their back – in the same order – saying each part out loud as I draw it: 'Here's the head, and then a big fat body, a wiggly tail, two ears and whiskers.' I then 'clean' the child's back and draw the cat again, this time missing out one of the elements. The child has to guess which bit I've missed out.

I do this a few times, each time being very positive with the child about how well they're doing. It's not important for them to know if they've got it right or not (that's just helpful information for me and the parents – that is, knowing whether the child can do it and, if they can't, how to grade any work they do on this so that the child is getting a challenge that is only just beyond what they can comfortably manage). I want the child to leave the session feeling as if they've done brilliantly, and keen to get started when they get home.

ELSA AND SEAN: PART 2 – RESPONDING TO TOUCH, AND NEXT STEPS IN ASSESSING DISCRIMINATION

ELSA

As you might have predicted, Elsa was really good at this and enjoyed it. It's always helpful to be able to find, as part of the assessment, things that children enjoy and succeed in – they can be so useful to pepper any programme with so the child knows that there are some of the games that they're experts at. I find that these sorts of drawing on your back games are also a lovely way to be close and playful. So while Elsa wasn't really needing to do things like this to build discriminatory function, we used it as a nice relationship-building game and a good 'break' from the more challenging games she was going to be doing.

SEAN

I didn't do this with Sean, because it was clear that he was over-responsive to light touch, so instead we went back a stage and played a game with firmer pressure. Still with Sean lying on his tummy across his mum's knee, I asked his mum to pat out two familiar tunes on his back – I think it was a very seasonal 'Jingle Bells' and 'When Santa Got Stuck Up the Chimney'– and to see if he could discern which one she was doing. He was quite good at this, which gave us a great starting point for work. Using firmer pressure was much more settling for his system.

Part 3: Building up a picture of discriminatory tactile functioning

Taste games

I tend to use crisps for this – just because they're pretty portable and most children like them. I sometimes use bags of chocolate buttons that have got white and milk chocolate in them, or red and green grapes or other fruits – anything that has the same texture but tastes different is fine. It's always important to make sure that the child likes and feels comfortable with whatever I'm using. If I can't find anything they like, then I'll suggest that the parents try at home with food they know the child enjoys.

If I'm using crisps, I start by asking the child what flavours of crisps they like and choosing two of those. (I generally have five or six flavours in my bag, but most children choose ready salted, cheese and onion or salt and vinegar. I try not to use prawn cocktail crisps because their colour is so distinctive). I put a handful of the crisps into three bowls – two bowls have the same flavour and one has a different flavour. (If you're going to try this, do a bit of market research first and make sure that the crisps you're using do actually taste very different from each other. I've used many different brands over the years and have been surprised that some have been remarkably similar to each other. However, you don't want them to be overpoweringly strong either, just different enough for the chid to be able to discern difference.)

With younger children, I usually try and make this into more of a game. I say that we're going to pretend there's a crisp factory opening in their town, and that today is their interview to become chief crisp taster in the factory. To start, I give the child a crisp from the first bowl and ask them to taste that, seeing if their tongue and mouth can give them clues about what it is. I then give them a crisp that's a different flavour and ask them to taste that one and to say if they think it is the same or different.

The first thing to notice at this stage is how the child manages the task. For some children, just having a small bowl of crisps in front of them is too much and they gobble the lot before I've even had time to tell them what we're doing. Others eat the crisps by chewing them with their teeth like wood going through a planer and then swallowing, so not really tasting at all. Others throw the crisp to the back of their mouth and swallow, again not really tasting.

All of this is really useful information about the child's relationship to food and eating, and really helpful in finding the right starting point for work.

For children who are able to put the crisp into their mouth and have a moment of consideration before they swallow it, I'm interested to see whether they can discern same or different. After they've tried the two different flavours, I present the third bowl and say that it's the same flavour as one of the ones they have already tried, wondering if they can find which one of the first two bowls that is the same.

If a child is really fast and good at this, I'll make it harder by getting them to close their eyes, giving them two crisps to put in their mouth at the same time and asking if they can tell if I've given them two different flavours or two crisps that are the same flavour. This is definitely one to try yourself.

ELSA AND SEAN: PART 3 – TASTE
ELSA
Elsa had quite an extreme reaction to this game – she found the taste of the salt and vinegar crisps much too tangy. Her system was over-responsive to the flavour and her parents said that at home she could only tolerate the blandest of food. Now it may be that Elsa is someone who is always going to like quite bland food, but because her reaction was so out of the ordinary, we agreed that it would be good to see if there were any ways of working on this to widen her repertoire and enjoyment of different foods and flavours.

SEAN
Sean, however, was a great taster. He could tell me straightaway not only that the first two were different from each other, but which flavours and brand they were. His mum and dad said that Sean enjoyed a good range of flavours at home but struggled to chew things like meat and didn't like a lot of texture. So while Elsa and Sean presented very differently in this task, both had parts of this system that we could try to improve.

When I'm doing this part of the assessment, it's important to ask about food and eating at home and the child's relationship with food. Parents can usually say whether their child is using food to fill an emotional gap or whether their eating looks quite different from friends of their age. For example, if a child is ten and has a strong preference for food without lumps, or a very limited range of foods that they like, or takes a long time to eat, or struggles with chewing, I find that it is useful to put some different experiences of 'mouthly' activities alongside those early ones and start them off with some of the oral games to see if we can improve things a bit. I also notice things like whether the child is dribbling and whether their speech is clear and easy to understand. If a child's speech is indistinct or slurred and it forms part of a picture of an underdeveloped system, I'll think with the parents about trying to rebuild that system, perhaps before making a speech and language therapy referral.

Assessing the tactile system – a summary

The main things to be thinking about with the tactile system are defensive versus discriminatory function, on a physiological and an emotional level. As well as the mechanics of how the system is working, I want to notice whether the child is able to stay in the moment of the experience and manage the uncertainty of not knowing. Below I outline the indicators for a child with an underdeveloped tactile system.

Discriminatory tactile functioning

- Very sensitive to touch, for example gets very giddy and overexcited with even the lightest touch.

- Under-sensitive to touch, for example doesn't register touch. At home, parents might talk about their child not noticing pain when they've fallen or are injured.

Defensive tactile functioning

- Needs to be in charge and in control at all times, for example when playing a game always has to be the one who makes the rules, reluctant to let anyone else decide what game and how it is played.

- Constantly watchful and hypervigilant. Children in this state of mind often hear things that others may just filter out, like noticing the sound of a bus going past in the next street, in a way that interferes with focus and concentration.

- Unable to stay in the moment of an experience and manage the uncertainty of not knowing – perhaps always needing to know what's happening and when it's happening – and hating the feeling of not knowing something.

Oral functioning

- Dribbles more than their peers, perhaps when eating or speaking, or just generally.

- Has speech or singing that is hard to understand.

- Finds chewing effortful, for example when eating un-processed meat (like a roast rather than a sausage).

- Constantly seeks out things to chew.

- Gravitates towards soft food that doesn't take much effort to eat.

- Doesn't seem to taste food, for example might eat so fast that they can't tell what they're eating, or just seems to throw the food to the back of their mouth and swallow.

Other useful resources

Before we move onto the kinds of games and activities that I find useful in rebuilding underdeveloped tactile systems, there are some other resources that are helpful when thinking about limbic systems and regulation. Ruby Jo Walker has developed a great online resource outlining polyvagal theory on one page of A4 paper.[1] She talks about 'calm connectedness', which I like because it allows for the connectedness to be with ourselves on a bodily level as well as with people or even ideas or other things. It's in this

---

1   www.rubyjowalker.com

state of mind that we have that endless potential – to play, think, feel, remember, learn, relate.

Beacon House is an organization offering clinical services and training around trauma. It has a multidisciplinary team who have developed some fantastic online resources[2] – one of my favourites is their film about the 'Window of Tolerance' where they describe the idea of the child retreating to a space where they feel safe and need an adult to join them there and help them to expand that space. The graphics are great and it really captures the sense of starting where the child is and moving with them from there.

Eadaoin Bhreathnach is an OT who has developed the Sensory Attachment Intervention and written a series of books, *The Scared Gang* (Bhreathnach 2011), that contain a wealth of ideas and information especially helpful in thinking about levels of arousal and strategies for regulation.

---

2   http://beaconhouse.org.uk

Chapter 7

Ideas for Rebuilding Underdeveloped Tactile Systems: Touch

IN Chapter 5, we thought about the tactile system evolving from one that's primed for survival in the newborn (*defensive functioning*) to one that evolves, through repeated experiences of love and nurture, to enable the child to stay in the moment of an experience and for there to be space within that moment for the child to play, relate and learn without being overwhelmed by anxiety or fear – what we think of in tactile terms as good *discriminatory functioning*. This evolution is both bodily and psychological, and paying attention to both of these elements is what makes this such an important system when working with children who have had significant gaps in their early experiences. In this chapter, I focus on both physiological and emotional aspects. However, it's important to know that this is to make it easier to consider rebuilding an underdeveloped system, rather than it being an accurate description of how the system develops.

Just as we did in the assessment, we focus on three parts of the tactile system when rebuilding an underdeveloped tactile system:

- Touch, where the child is doing the touching and trying to discern what they're touching.

- Touch, where the child is being touched.

- Taste and oral functioning – we'll look at this in Chapter 8.

When I'm doing any activities to rebuild underdeveloped systems, my starting point is always the child's state of mind, thinking of that continuum from defensive to discriminatory functioning and making changes and adaptations along the way if the child seems to be shifting from one state to another. I meet children who have islands of good discriminatory functioning – maybe they'll have managed all the games in this part of the assessment really easily – but I know from parents/school that there are times when they get much more stressed and it's much harder for them to be in the moment of an experience. If I think there's any room for things to be better and for them to be more able to stay tuned in to the moment of an experience (as well as the actual functioning of the system), then I'll generally suggest that we include some of the games from this tactile system in the first few weeks of work. These kinds of games and activities can be so helpful in building relationships and helping parents to feel themselves to be key to setting up the environment in which the child is going to succeed, that it feels a bit remiss not to include them. I don't think I've ever given a family a programme of work that hasn't included one or two games for this system.

Again, it's important to pitch the activities at a level that's right for the parents as well as the child, because if, as parents, they're feeling a bit overwhelmed and have had a run of feeling that what they've been doing has not been working, then it's important to use activities that will be fun and engaging for the child but will also help the parents to regain a sense of themselves as the agents of change and to get some fun and playfulness back into the relationship. If parents are really struggling, I'll work alongside other therapists to supplement this intervention. Where practitioners have had some level of training, the BUSS model fits really well into frameworks like the Golding and Hughes (2012) PACE (playfulness, acceptance, curiosity and empathy) work and DDP (Hughes, Golding and Hudson 2019) as well as Theraplay® (Booth 2009) or filial therapy (Guerney and Ryan 2013; VanFleet 2013).

Getting the 'just right' challenge

When I'm trying to work out the right level of challenge for a child and family, I keep the idea of a ladder in my head for each activity. The way the activity is presented in the assessment is like the midpoint of the ladder; the steps above increase the level of challenge, while the steps below make it easier.

When we're climbing up a ladder, we usually keep one foot on the rung we're on, and move the other foot onto the next rung up. We don't tend to go from the bottom rung to the fifth rung in one step, and it's useful to think of gently moving a child onto the next (or an earlier) step of the ladder one stage at a time.

Thinking a bit more about a 'just right' challenge, I mean an activity that's at the right level for that individual child. For children who are anxious or cautious of this activity, the right challenge might mean making the activity easily achievable, because what I aim to do is to build an association between a feeling of well-being and enjoyment with this game – not wanting to stretch the child, just to get them comfortable with playing it to start with. For another child, the 'just right' challenge might mean pitching the game at the level just slightly above the one they're functioning at – too far above their current level and it'll be too difficult; just keeping to what they can already do and they'll get bored very quickly. This probably makes it sound a bit harder than it really is – we all do this sort of thing all of the time without even thinking about it. Think of something like learning to get dressed – parents are experts in knowing how to grade this, starting with the child doing the part of the process they think they'll succeed at and gradually working up from there. Or when the child is learning to zip up their coat – parents generally know how long is 'just right' so that the child has a go at it and the chance of doing it, but not so long that they get really frustrated, take the coat off, throw it on the floor and stomp off upstairs.

It's about getting the point of stepping in or offering words of encouragement that help to keep it in the 'just right' zone.

The level of 'just right' challenge may be completely different for two children who were both able to discern the objects in the feely bag game. If the challenge only fits the practical skill and not the state of mind the child is in, or the parent–child relationship, it won't be a 'just right' challenge for that child.

Part 1: Using touch to increase discriminatory and decrease defensive tactile functioning – the child doing the touching

The following games are a useful starting point and ones that I use frequently with families.

- Feely bag game and variations.

- Jigsaw game and variations.

- Other games to build discrimination.

If you're a parent, and feel confident trying some of these ideas with your own child, I've given details about how to grade them so that you can try and get the level of challenge right. We'll think again about Sean and Elsa and how they progressed through each of the parts.

Feely bag game

I've already gone into detail in Chapter 6 about how to set up and play the feely bag game in the assessment stage. Here I just want to think about how I grade the activity so that I can try and get the 'just right' challenge for each child. In a nutshell, there are three variables: how many objects are in the bag, how similar they are to each other and who is in charge of the game.

To make the game easier

How to make it easier will, of course, depend on why the child is finding it hard, so I'll try to cover all bases. Ideas about how to make things simpler (or more complex) always work best when they are considered by parents or carers as they know their children really well and can decide what will be suitable for them. With these modifications, I'm assuming a combination of difficulties with discriminatory functioning as well as feeling anxious and needing to be in control.

One step back – reduce the number of objects in the bag. As a starting point from the original feely bag, I tend to take the smaller objects out. Once the child is able to find these things quickly and accurately with their dominant hand, ask them to use their non-dominant hand. When they can do this too, move up to having more things in the bag and work your way up the ladder.

Sometimes this can take a while, and it's helpful if families can keep changing the contents of the bag to stop the game getting boring. I'm a big fan of sneaking in a treat or a surprise from time to time – just an unexpected bonus like a little sweet or a very small toy.

All the time I notice how the child does each part of the activity:

- Is it easy?

- Do they do it quickly?

- Are they accurate in what they're finding?

- Are they still rushing to do it? Is being quick still more important than getting it right?

- I'm also noticing whether the child is just using the tips of their fingers to find things or if they are really moulding their hand around the object to feel it.

I keep adapting the game in response to these observations. It's important to note that progress doesn't have to be linear; some children can jump around between the stages if that's what's most helpful for them.

Two steps back – make the objects very different from each other. If the child is able to tolerate not knowing what's in the bag, has got an idea that this is going to be fun and they'll be able to do it, but just struggles to discriminate between the different items, then it's helpful to make sure the objects are all very different. This time the bag might contain a Playmobil® figure, a piece of Lego®, a door key, a pom pom and a pencil.

Three steps back – if the child is struggling even with a small number of very different toys, then it can be useful to try and work out if the difficulty is with the discriminatory touch itself or about not being in charge or not being able to manage the uncertainty of not knowing. If the problem seems to be primarily with discriminatory touch, then I encourage parents and carers to highlight touch and a different sensation as many times a day as possible, for a week or so. For example, if they're supporting the child when they're getting dressed in the morning, I might suggest seeing if the child can close their eyes and guess whether what they've passed them is their socks or their pants, or their sweatshirt or their t-shirt. I want to help the child to tune in to everyday sensation and help their body become more aware. I suggest they do it with weight as well; for example when dinner is being made, trying to guess which item they think is going to be heaviest – the jar of sauce or the bag of pasta, the bag of potatoes or the bag of sweetcorn – then weighing them and seeing whether they are right. This can be a fun game to play at the supermarket, on a day when there's a bit of extra time – which is heavier, the butternut squash or the turnip? With these games, we're trying to help the child to tune in to what they're touching and holding and to start to notice its properties.

If the difficulties seem to be more about the child struggling with not being in charge or being able to manage not knowing, then I take another step back down the ladder.

Four steps back – who is in charge? I want us to get to the point where the child feels comfortable with the grown-up being in charge of both what goes into the feely bag and what the child is looking for, and for some children this can take a while. There are times when this grading has to be done in stages, perhaps taking turns of who chooses or who puts the objects in the bag – whatever is needed until there's a shift and the child is able to trust that it is going to be alright, and that they're feeling confident doing it. If the child is doing this game in different settings, perhaps at home and school, it's important to ensure good communication between settings.

SEAN: FIRST STEPS IN REBUILDING DISCRIMINATION

Sean, who you'll remember just couldn't wait to know what was in the bag and, even when he did know, wasn't getting good enough messages from his hands about what he was feeling, started here. His family made a nice, big bag and Sean would find four of his toys to put inside it and they'd play from there. They played it several times a day and his parents found that he only needed to stay at this level for a few days before they shifted it so they were finding the things to put in the bag. By this time, Sean was very comfortable with the game and really enjoyed the 'not knowing' and trying to guess what it might be. They played this so many times that it was only a few more days before they could increase the number of objects they were using.

To make the game harder

There are lots of different ways to do this. I generally increase the number of objects and then how similar they are to each other (but not both at once).

One step forward – try adding a few more things into the bag and asking the child to find them with both their dominant and non-dominant hand. It's good to keep things playful and fun, so I usually introduce a dialogue like, 'Okay, for the next one, do you want to try easy, hard or super hard?' That way I notice how the child is feeling about how they're doing and I can use this to know how carefully I need to be grading it or if I need to be staying at this level.

ELSA: USING FEELY BAGS TO BUILD CONFIDENCE

Even though it was clear from Elsa's assessment that she had islands of good discriminatory functioning, her confidence was much lower, and so we decided that the family would continue to play the feely bag game at the same level. Her parents kept changing the range of objects in the bag but without it getting too much harder –it seemed more important to try and get some playfulness going and for Elsa to be feeling she was really good at it, than to increase the complexity. As you'll see in Chapter 15, when I met with Elsa's parents four weeks after the first assessment to review progress, they talked about how much fun they were having with this and how important it was to have something in the programme that Elsa felt herself to be good at, and how this balanced out the physical challenges of the vestibular and proprioceptive activities they were doing.

Two steps forward – increase complexity by adding even more things, but make sure that that they are similar in some way to things that are already in the bag. So if there's a pencil in there, I might add a pencil with a rubber on the end, or if there's a biro in there, I might add a biro with a lid – things that feel the same but are also a bit different. Or maybe a large marble and a golf ball, or two bracelets, one made of glass beads and one of wooden beads.

Three steps forward – finding two objects at the same time. The child puts both their hands into the bag and tries to find duplicate items (for example, both hands find a battery) or similar shapes (for example, the left hand finds a golf ball and the right hand finds a marble).

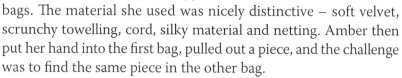

Four steps forward – two bags/two hands. It's fun to make a duplicate bag – the same size bag with exactly the same things in each. This time the child has to put a hand in each bag and find the same thing at the same time.

Five steps forward – material feely bags. This was devised by Amber's mum (we'll meet Amber in Chapter 9) and is a great way of making this game even harder. Amber's mum cut up lots of different pieces of material and put a copy of each into two bags. The material she used was nicely distinctive – soft velvet, scrunchy towelling, cord, silky material and netting. Amber then put her hand into the first bag, pulled out a piece, and the challenge was to find the same piece in the other bag.

Amber got really good at this game and her mum made it even harder by putting four pieces of each kind of material in the bag: one that she'd cut with pinking shears so it had a zig-zag edge, one that she'd cut with a straight edge, one that was cut into a circle shape and one that was cut into a triangle shape. Amber had to find not only the right fabric, but also the right cut as well.

NADIA: NOT WANTING TO FALL OVER AT PLAYTIME

We'll talk about this more when we come on to think about proprioceptive functioning, but I just want to mention children who struggle to know where their feet are and how some of the games from the tactile system can help with this. One such child was Nadia, who was six when I met her and her adoptive parents (Nadia's mum talks about her experience of using the BUSS model in Chapter 17). When I met them, Nadia was falling over a lot, at home and at school. Her mum noticed one day that Nadia had come home with lots of little stones in her shoes and saw that her feet looked sore not only from the stones but also from where she'd pulled the Velcro on her shoes much too tightly. She asked Nadia about this, who explained that the stones and fastening her shoes so tightly helped her to know where her feet were, so that she wouldn't fall over as much when she was playing with her friends. (Nadia was the first child I'd met who was doing this, but I've since met quite a few more who do similar things to try and sort out the problems they know they're having. It always strikes me as being both ingenious and very sad at the same time.)

To help Nadia's brain and central nervous system build up a picture of where her feet were without her having to feel the pain of the stones in her shoes, as well as doing lots of proprioceptive work, we played the jigsaw game, which is really an extension of the feely bag game, as well as lots of other 'feely' games to help increase awareness of her feet and what they were doing. I'm really pleased to say that this worked quickly and Nadia didn't have to keep filling her shoes with stones.

The jigsaw game

Materials needed:

- Big foam jigsaw pieces.

- Different pieces of fabric.

For Nadia, to begin with, it was important to use a range of fabrics that were different and distinct from each other. I suggested Nadia's mum use an old towel that had been dried outside and so was stiff and hard, some soft, fleecy material, an old plastic bag, an old jute bag, cord, denim, an old cotton shirt that had got quite soft with use, a silky fabric and an old jumper.

To make the game

Nadia's mum cut the fabric to fit the jigsaw pieces and glued it onto them. She kept a duplicate of each piece and put it into a little bag. To play the game, Nadia took her socks off, put on a blindfold and put her hand into the bag and pulled out one piece of fabric. She felt this and then walked across the jigsaw pieces, trying to match the piece of fabric that she was feeling in her hand with one she was walking over with her bare feet.

As she got better at this, her mum made it harder by having fabric that was more similar and increasing the number of pieces in the jigsaw.

Other games the BUSS model uses to build discrimination

The following ideas are based on the feely bag game.

In a bath with lots of bubbles – Percy's mum, who'll you'll meet in Chapter 17, devised this. The idea here is to hide things under the bubbles for a child to find. She found that this was a good step before the feely bag because Percy struggled to manage the length of time it took to put his hand into the bag and then start finding things.

In a sand pit – again, this involves hiding things for the child to find. It's fun to give clues by telling the child if they're getting 'warmer' (closer to the object) or 'cooler' (further away from the object).

Lucky dip – you might remember these from your childhood. I don't know if they're still around, but when I was growing up a great game at a party or fair was to have a container with sawdust or polystyrene chips in it, with toys hidden in it. You just put your hand in and felt around until you found something to pull out.

Part 2: Using touch to increase discriminatory and decrease defensive tactile functioning – the child being touched

The *roller ball game* and the *drawing on a child's back* form the basis for the assessment of this system (see Chapter 6), but are also helpful in rebuilding this system. It's useful to separate out the child's emotional and physical responses to being touched because it gives a good clue about where to start. I often meet young people whose early experiences of being touched have been frightening and painful, and for these young people we need to start with their emotional response to being touched, even though we know this will be wrapped up with their physical response. It's important, in my experience, for them to be in control of how we progress. I tend to start by thinking with them about their relationship with touch and being touched and asking if they'd like to do some work on it so that it gets a bit easier. Sometimes they're happy to start with the games that involve them doing the touching, but other times they're just not ready, and if they don't want to think about it or work on it, then I don't proceed any further.

If they are happy to continue, then I go back through the agreement we made in the being touched part of the assessment, making sure that we practise how the child will let me or their parents know that they want us to stop. I usually make sure we've got a gesture as well as a verbal sign. Then I proceed at the pace of the young person, all the time watching and talking with them about how I'm pacing it and whether it feels okay.

RORY: WORKING SLOWLY TOWARDS TOUCH

Rory is a 14-year-old boy whose early history of abuse and neglect had left him quite cut off from his body and wary of being touched. When I met with his foster carer to talk about the assessment and what we'd be doing, she very helpfully told me that Rory 'didn't do touch' and it was clear that she was very wary of touching him in case she upset him. When I met Rory, I changed the order in which I did the assessment, so that we'd already done most of the games and activities before I came to the being touched part of things. The rest of the assessment had gone well; Rory was curious about himself and interested in my understanding of why he was finding things like riding his bike or writing difficult, and was engaged in the idea of rebuilding the underdeveloped parts of his systems to see if we could get his body working any better. It's important to say that if the assessment hadn't been going well and I hadn't felt that I'd been able to get a good working relationship going with Rory, I'd have finished things there and suggested we meet again in a week or so when he'd had some time to think about the things we'd done so far.

But because it was going well, and because I knew that his foster carer (who was with us) was really perceptive, I felt confident that she would be able to continue anything we started that day, and also be very well able to notice and take care of him if he did find things a bit unsettling. These are very important caveats, and are reasons that I tend not to do assessments in school. I'm not assessing the child in isolation, I'm interested in the child within their family or care setting, because all of those things are going to influence how we proceed. It's back to that same Winnicottian idea (1957) of there being no such thing as a baby, just a nursing couple.

I told Rory that the next part of the assessment was a bit like the taste test, in that we would be seeing how well his body made sense of signals from outside his body – so we were looking at taste in the crisp test, and here we'd be looking at how he registered touch. Rory seemed curious, but I was cautious about rushing on and him then finding us doing something that he hadn't really bargained for and didn't really like. So I talked more about how I'd like to see if his body could accurately 'decode' messages from outside his body, and I demonstrated by using the roller ball on my forearm, drawing a circle. I showed him (still on my arm) how I was going to draw a circle followed by a rectangle and then ask him to look away and see if he could work out what the shape was without using his eyes. He was happy with this but again I reiterated (and we practised again) how he could tell me to stop at any time. There are times when this feels a bit convoluted and as if it takes ages, but I'd much rather proceed cautiously and with the young person knowing that they are in charge of things, rather than rushing in.

So, we started with me making a shape with the ball on Rory's arm, over his school jumper. We did this a number of times, with me making it more complex as he got more comfortable with it. He was pretty good at naming the shape! The next step was supporting his foster carer in feeling comfortable playing this game so that they could carry on at home, so we did the whole thing over again (right back to the 'how to stop' part) and started the drawing part, with Rory drawing the shapes on his foster carer's arm, and then with his foster carer drawing the shapes on his arm. We agreed they'd practise this (and a few other things!) and that I'd meet with them in a month to see how they were getting on.

When we met again a month later I was pleased that they had not only kept on doing it, but had also come up with all sorts of interesting extensions themselves (from hand massages to an elaborate circle game that they played as a family). Rory's foster carer also said how nice it was that Rory had become much more affectionate, asking for hugs and giving her hugs (Rory was carefully studying his phone in a very age-appropriate way as she told me this!).

The roller ball and drawing on back games

The games of rolling the ball on the palm of a child's hand and on their back usually provide useful information about whether the child is over- or under-responsive to touch. When I'm suggesting that families use this game at home to rebuild an underdeveloped system, the starting point for children who are under- and over-responsive to touch is the same. This might sound a bit counter-intuitive at first, but what's needed in both cases is firmer touch, which will either settle or awaken the system. You'll recognize that this is how I graded Sean's assessment and I thought it might be helpful here to explain in a bit more detail how and why I did it like that.

SEAN: BUILDING DISCRIMINATORY TACTILE FUNCTIONING

It can help to settle our central nervous systems if we lie on our tummies rather than sitting up to do an activity (again we'll think more about this when we move on to the vestibular and proprioceptive systems). So with younger children who are over-responding to touch, I tend to ask parents to sit down on the sofa and get the child into a comfortable position lying across their knee, with the child on their tummy.

With Sean, a cushion under his tummy made this more comfortable, but other children just like to prop themselves up on their arms – either is fine. If a child is under-responsive to touch, it can still help to do it like this, but it isn't as important as it is for children who are over-responsive to touch.

From the position of the child lying over their parent's knee, I ask parents to move away from the kind of light touch that you get with the roller ball and to use firmer pressure. This is achieved by using a flat hand, so there is a much greater surface area of the child's back being touched, and the pressure needs to be just firm enough for the child to feel that they're being touched. I usually demonstrate this, using the parent's back, so that they can feel what it's like.

Sean's parents used Christmas songs, but if parents think that nursery rhymes will be easiest for their child, then they will need two that have quite different rhythms, like 'Twinkle Twinkle Little Star' and 'Hickory Dickory Dock'. For the first time doing this, I ask the parent to sing the nursery rhyme while they pat it out on their child's back, then the second time, just to introduce the songs and then do the patting. Just as we did with Sean, the third time I ask the parents not to tell the child which of the two songs they're going to do, and just pat out the rhythm of one, seeing if the child is able to guess which it is.

Once they were home, Sean's parents found that the more they did this, the more Sean was able to stay lying still and tune in to what they were doing, and got better and better at discerning the songs they were tapping out. They were able to make it harder by using songs that had fairly similar rhythms to each other – at least for the first part – so that they were extending the time Sean had to 'listen' before he'd be able to guess the answer.

We talked about the next steps – to try drawing on his back again with much firmer strokes and from there to move from drawing with him lying on their knees to him lying on the sofa beside them and then sitting up.

To make the game harder

There are so many ways to go forward with these games and I encourage parents just to have fun with them. Drawings on the child's back can get more complex – sometimes it helps to have a 'theme' such as weather, animals or pieces of furniture, anything that is familiar to the child and makes it fun and interesting for them. But often families get so good at this that they're drawing really complicated pictures on each other's backs and guessing brilliantly – so I usually encourage them to just go for it and have fun!

Other (mostly parent-inspired) ideas around touch games

- Hand massages and nail painting.

- Clapping games.

- Lap games – like 'Round and round the garden' – these can be good to play on the child's hand, back and, if they're not too ticklish, their feet.

Chapter 8

Ideas for Rebuilding Underdeveloped Tactile Systems: Taste and Oral Games

W E'VE already thought about the idea of building regulation through relationship, and relationship through regulation, and nowhere is this as important as when we're thinking about the oral systems. I always welcome the opportunity to lay down new experiences of nurture, being fed emotionally and physically, alongside those early feeding and weaning ones, as well as building oral strength and, of course, building discriminatory functioning! It's a lot to do, but it's usually good fun and there are lots of opportunities for families to be creative.

The taste test in the assessment gives a surprising amount of information for such a simple activity. As we discussed in Chapter 6, it is possible get a good feel of the child's relationship with food by seeing how they go about this task and noticing the process as well as the end point. The sorts of things that suggest that there may be capacity to improve functioning in this system include:

- A child who is struggling to discern flavours.

- Carers who are describing a very restricted diet.

- A child who is taking a very long time to eat and/or eating seems more effortful than you'd expect. Parents often describe children struggling to chew pieces of meat (I've not worked out the vegetarian equivalent to this – meat is such a handy way of noticing oral strength!).

• Difficulty in understanding a child's speech or the articulation isn't as clear as it needs to be for a child to make themselves understood.

• A child who is still producing a lot of saliva beyond the stage you'd expect that.

• Descriptions of children who are doing a lot of chewing at home or at school (as Lenny was, chewing his way through his school coat when he was anxious).

There are other times when I just use these games because they're fun, good for building relationships and, if I'm asking families to work on systems that are really quite underdeveloped, it can be good to have a bit of light relief and for a child to have something that they feel themselves to be really good at. So even if a child has been excellent at discerning flavours, it might still be worth doing some of these games. Sometimes it's parents who are in need of some light relief – I often meet families where the parents are quite worn down and have had lots of advice from many different people, so it can be helpful just to start things off by having fun and everyone experiencing some success.

Once I've established that we're going to do some work on this part of the system, I need to get more information. I'll know a bit from the assessment about the discerning of different flavours and can build on that, but I need to get more information about oral strength and stamina, and this is where straws come in very handy!

The games
The milk challenge

This is another game that's good to have tried yourself, and also to have road tested with a number of typically developing children of different ages, so that you've got an idea of how easy/difficult it is. This is always important in understanding the significance of what you see in a child. I find that working or living with children who have experienced developmental trauma can give a very skewed idea of developmental norms. I remember asking a large group of adoptive parents what age they thought typically developing children could walk down stairs, one foot to each step, without holding on. After quite a lot of discussion, the general consensus of the room was between nine and ten, because that was slightly older than their children, none of whom could manage it yet. In fact between two and three is more typical. So it's really good to keep immersing yourself in norms of development, both as a way of understanding variation but also because we want to support these children to get to as close to normal as we can – remembering all the time this is an underdeveloped rather than a broken system.

Equipment needed:

- A tall glass.

- Two straws – just regular straws, not those little ones you get on juice cartons or the curly ones you can buy. Metal and paper straws work well, although if a child is struggling with sucking or producing too much saliva, then paper ones get soggy too quickly.

- Milk (assuming the child likes/can drink milk. If not, it needs to be something that's a bit thicker than water but not too thick).

We sit at a table for this activity. I ask parents to pour a couple of centimetres of milk into a glass and ask the child to blow bubbles in the milk until they get the milk all the way to the top of the glass but to stop before it spills over the top.

If a child can do this easily, we can move straight on to the next level; but if this seems to take a lot of effort, then we need to make it easier, and can do this by either putting more milk into the glass or by giving the child another straw.

Putting this information together with the taste test, we begin to get a picture of discernment and oral strength and, depending on the results, the next stage is to plan activities to help build either one or both parts of this system.

SEAN: THE MILK CHALLENGE

Sean's mum sent me a video of Sean doing the milk game. I could see how hard he was finding it – his mum had helpfully put about 4 cm of milk in the glass and, even with quite a lot of milk, it took lots of 'puffs' to get the milk to the top of the glass. What was lovely to see (and hear) was the great encouragement Sean was getting from the rest of the family – really helping him to feel that he was doing a brilliant job! They kept doing this a few times a day and Sean was delighted at how much better he got at it.

Building discernment

It's important to reiterate that, at this stage of things, I'm not trying to increase the repertoire of foods that the child is eating (it is hoped that this will come later), so it's important to use food that the child likes and feels comfortable eating – no surprises! It all needs to be very predictable and to move at the child's pace. Sometimes carers talk about how hard it can be to persuade their child to try anything new or different and then I suggest trying to do this with a bit more stealth – rather than setting it up as a game, try weaving these kind of activities into everyday life, but always choose moments when you think the child is in a state of mind that might allow a little moment of playfulness. An example of this might be a nice day out where the family are having ice creams. Instead of all getting the same flavour, I'd suggest a few different (and distinct) ones that the family think the child might like – perhaps strawberry with bits of fruit in it alongside chocolate or lemon sorbet – whatever might work for that child on that day! Then each person takes a turn closing their eyes, trying each of them and seeing if they can guess which flavour is which. Sometimes introducing these sorts of tasting games at times like this, so they are associated with fun times, can be a good starting point. And as long as parents or carers can hold on to this and try and build on it when they're home (or the next time they're out) it can be helpful.

To make this easier

If a child is struggling here, I always pair these games with the blowing and sucking straw games, just to give this system as much input as we can.

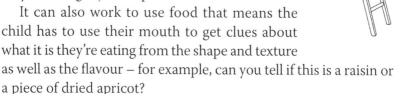

One step back – increase the difference in texture of the food a little bit – so rather than using crisps, which have the same texture, I introduce food where the texture is a little, but not wildly, different. So if the child is able to tolerate not seeing what they're being given to eat, I encourage parents to make a piece of toast, spreading each half with two things the child likes, perhaps one half with peanut butter and one half with jam. They then cut each half up into bite-sized pieces and see if the child can discern whether the one they're eating is jam or peanut butter.

It can also work to use food that means the child has to use their mouth to get clues about what it is they're eating from the shape and texture as well as the flavour – for example, can you tell if this is a raisin or a piece of dried apricot?

This is where we started with Elsa, who you'll remember was very sensitive to the strong flavour of the salt and vinegar crisps we used at the assessment. We did this alongside lots of sucking and blowing games to try and recalibrate that very oversensitive response to what Elsa was eating.

Two steps back – if this is still hard for the child to discern, then the next step back is to use food where the difference in texture is greater. So, can you tell if this is a piece of apple or a piece of orange? A piece of banana or a piece of carrot? A piece of crunchy pepper or a grape?

Three steps back – this involves another increase in difference, and here I find it's necessary to use food that gives a lot of sensory feedback. If children are under-responding to the flavours, then to try and tell the difference between things like sherbet or popping candy, grapes that have been frozen, a mouthful of fresh bread or a spoonful of natural yogurt, is a good challenge. They're distinct from each other in taste and texture, so should be easier to tell apart. Then, as we with the touch games, I suggest to families that they keep practising until it's easy for the child and they can move back up the ladder, just step by step as capacity increases.

To make this harder

One step forward – there are lots of ways to do this, but I suggest to families that they try and hold in mind the idea of either increasing the number of flavours or how similar they are to each other – just not both at once. To increase the range of flavours with crisps, I simply add in more flavours and see if the child can correctly identify the one they're eating. There are so many flavours of crisps on the market that it can be tempting to get a bit carried away, but remember to stick with what the child likes!

The other way to work on this is to have foods that are similar to each other in some way (often texture) but that are different too – so, for example, trying to discern different colours of grapes and peppers, or a pea and piece of sweetcorn.

Two steps forward – giving a child two different flavours of something at the same time and seeing if they can discern what they are is a lot trickier but can be good fun and it's quite easy to rein it back in a bit if it's too ambitious. I did this at a training session recently, with milk chocolate and white chocolate buttons. Everyone was convinced that they would be able to tell which they were eating and that, if I gave them two at the same time, they'd be able to tell if they were the same, or if it was one milk and one white chocolate button. Try it yourself – it's surprisingly hard. (I think that this is a feature of growing up – I've yet to meet a typically developing teenager who can't do it really easily.)

It is of course easier using flavours that are very different and distinct to each other, so jam and peanut butter are easier than using raspberry jam and strawberry jam. If we go back to the toast example, instead of giving the child one square of the toast and seeing if they can guess if it's peanut butter or jam, give them two pieces together and see if they can discern whether you've given them the same flavour on both or one of each.

Building oral strength and stamina

Bring on the straws! Before I started to be interested in this, I had no idea that the world of straws was such a varied one. Different apertures, different lengths, different shapes – there is an endless variety, which gives endless possibilities for games. There are lots of environmentally friendly alternatives to plastic straws that are often better for our purpose because they're a bit more robust: wheat straws, bamboo straws…the list goes on.

To begin, I suggest families get a small range of straws, so that they can work out the 'just right' challenge for that child – so some of the more regular-sized ones, as well as some that are wider and some that are smaller. Sometimes, novelty straws in different shapes and colours keep things interesting as children's oral strength increases. The best ones I found went from the drink, up around the child's face like a pair of glasses, round the eyes and then into their mouth. Sadly they were quite short-lived because they were a nightmare to clean, but by that time they had served their function in terms of being engaging and entertaining!

My starting point for straw games is the milk game – once a child is able to blow bubbles up to the top of the glass of milk, then it's time to move on, and there are so many things you can move on to! I'll give a selection here but do get creative – just remember the idea of the 'just right' challenge!

Bubble mountain

This was taught to me by Lenny's mum and is a favourite with lots of families.

Equipment needed:

- washing-up bowl (or similar)
- water

- washing-up liquid

- straws

- optional extra – food colouring.

Put some water into the washing-up bowl and then add some washing-up liquid to that – make sure it's this way round and don't add the washing-up liquid at the same time as the water – we don't want any bubbles at this stage. Then give the straw to the child – their job is to blow into the water and make a bubble mountain. Lenny's mum found this was a good one to do with both her children together, as they could have competitions about who could blow the biggest mountain.

Adding food colouring gives a bit more interest, or sometimes schools I'm working with have done this using very watery paint mixed with PVA; they then made great prints by putting a piece of paper on top of the bowl at the end – very impressive!

Blow football
Equipment needed:

- ping pong ball

- straws

- something to be the goal.

This is a good one to play with both players lying on their tummies on a hard floor, because unless there's an 'edge' around the table, a lot of time is spent retrieving the ball from the floor! It doesn't really work on a carpet, so if carpet is the only floor covering, I suggest some plywood or something to make a smooth surface. Using the floor means that you've got lots of scope to increase or decrease the size of the pitch, depending on how easy or difficult this is for a child.

Blowing a ping pong ball around the bath

This probably doesn't need much explanation – a straw and a ping pong ball are all that are needed. To begin with, it's good to get an idea of how far they can blow the ball before parents or carers make it more challenging, perhaps giving them a course to go around – round the boat, past the duck…whatever you can come up with. As the child gets better at this, it's possible to add a bit of sucking too, with the child perhaps starting by sucking the ball up out of a bowl and ending by putting it in a boat. Families know what bath toys they've got and can get beautifully creative with this one!

Blowing a train

Blowing a train along a wooden track works too, and this can easily be made harder by adding in more track, corners and perhaps even an incline!

Drinking a yogurt with a straw

Sucking games – still with straws – are also great for building oral strength and stamina.

Once a child is able to blow bubbles in milk with an ordinary kind of straw and only a couple of centimetres of milk, I move them on to using a straw to eat things that they might normally use a spoon for. I grade this quite carefully, all the time wanting the child to succeed but also be challenged within the range they can manage. I start with a small pot of yogurt (without fruit pieces in it), seeing if the child is able to use their straw to suck it up rather than using a spoon to eat it. If this is hard, something like blancmange can be easier, or a smoothie, just to get started. Then to make it harder, I suggest they increase either the thickness of the food or how much they're drinking – so moving to a bigger pot of yogurt, or adding ice cream to a smoothie. One lad I saw recently got so good at this that he could use a straw to eat a little tub of jelly – very impressive!

Another way to increase the challenge is to move on to smaller straws. Sean's family would take their own (smaller) straws to McDonald's (other fast food outlets are available...) – the thick milkshakes were perfect for this task!

Often parents notice that activities like this, where the sucking is quite a challenge, can be a helpful calming activity.

LENNY, SEAN AND ELSA: BUILDING ORAL STRENGTH AND CREATING EXPERIENCES INVOLVING MOUTHLY GAMES, RELATIONSHIPS AND FUN

LENNY

We used lots of these games and activities with Lenny. I was wanting to give his parents a range of good, fun oral games that they could play together to put new experiences alongside the horribly neglectful and abusive ones he'd experienced as a baby and small boy (it felt a very underfed system that was eating its way through so many coats). I also wanted to build his oral strength and stamina and to help him to stay in the moment of an experience for a little bit longer, as well as using sucking as a good way of calming down. At home, the family played lots of the games I've described. At school, we worked out a series of 'sensory circuits' that Lenny could do at times of transition that were challenging. To begin with this was about five times a day: going into school in the morning; before whole class, carpet time teaching; coming in from playtime; coming in from lunchtime, and mid-afternoon. This included games to build vestibular and proprioceptive functioning that we'll come to in the next chapters, but school found that having Lenny suck yogurts through a straw while he was lying on his tummy was a very calming thing for him and really helped him to make the transition from zooming around in the playground to being in the quiet of the classroom.

SEAN

Sean really enjoyed all of these games too, and when I met with his parents four weeks after the initial assessment, they said that they were still having to do all of the blowing bubbles games because he was enjoying them so much but that he was now able to drink yogurts and milkshakes through straws. He had much greater oral strength and was able to stay with the challenge for increasing amounts of time.

ELSA

Elsa made a slower start with these, but moved on from the big straws to smaller ones in the milk game and was using a novelty straw to drink with most of the time. Her parents thought they could see a good shift in oral strength and in how much more comfortable Elsa seemed doing this and letting herself play around with it. We talked about introducing yogurts and obstacle courses over the coming weeks.

Chapter 9

The Vestibular System: The Foundation of All Systems

 YOU might remember the crane analogy from Chapter 1 – if we think of our body as being like a crane, then the vestibular system is the base of the crane. On a bodily level, we need a *stable base* or *core* from which we can perform increasingly complex tasks. For the developing baby, that stage of being up on their hands and knees and moving from having both hands down to being able to lift one hand off the ground and reach for something is a great example of the beginnings of this. The baby needs to contract all the muscles around their trunk to hold it in a good position while their arm is moving – beautiful co-contraction! If their middle is very wobbly, they are not able to accurately reach for the toy they are trying to get. Their body needs to know just which part it needs to move, and which parts need to be still to provide a base for the movement. If you watch a baby at this stage, you'll see lots of practice shots before they get this – lots of wobbling and overshooting of their movements while their body builds that stable core and their little system works out how much pressure or force is needed for the movement, but when they get there, it opens up the next chapter of development and they're almost ready to start moving.

On a bodily level, our base is our head, neck, shoulder girdle and trunk, often referred to as our core. This can be a bit confusing because people often forget about the head, neck and shoulders when they're thinking about a stable core and think of strong abdominals. However, we need to remember that the head and neck are a crucial part of the core! I worked with a foster carer recently who was mortified when she thought of all the times she had interpreted her foster child's head being down as her being disinterested or uncommunicative, only to realize that she had such low muscle tone she just couldn't hold it up all the time.

I've noticed over the years that there is quite a distinctive feel to these underdeveloped vestibular systems. When I first started working in this way I was really taken aback by just how low a child's muscle tone could feel. One foster carer said that he'd noticed, when he picked up his grandson, that it felt as if there was something holding him together around his middle, whereas, with the child he was looking after in placement, it felt as if his middle was made of overcooked spaghetti. Another foster carer described taking their foster child and one of her friends to the park, and lifting them each up onto a high platform. She was taken aback by the difference in the children. The friend's body seemed to be strong and helping her in the movement, whereas she felt as if she was lifting something very heavy and unyielding when she picked up her foster child, who was in fact, smaller and lighter than her friend.

The other fantastically important function that our vestibular system plays is *gravitational security*, and this divides into two parts. The first part, where the vestibular system works alongside the visual system, allows us to maintain a stable visual field while we're moving. Anyone who has had vertigo or suffered from inner ear infections will know how crucial this is – because without it, when we move it feels as if the whole world is moving with us in a way that is incredibly disorientating and makes us feel quite nauseous. If you're fortunate enough not to have suffered from these, you can sometimes get an idea of how the world would feel without our vestibular systems doing this for us when watching something like a wildlife documentary; those moments when the camera crew have been taken by surprise by something and start running show us a world that moves up and down with us as we move – really bumpy and jerky and quite disorientating. A high temperature can be enough to interfere with the working of the vestibular system and you're probably familiar with that lightheaded feeling you can get – a glimpse of how well our vestibular system works the rest of the time.

The second part of gravitational security is all about our feeling of connectedness and security with the ground, which may sound a bit strange to start with, but if you think for a moment how it feels if you do something like walk over a rope bridge and compare it with how it feels to be walking on flat, familiar ground, you can begin to get an idea of what I mean. My family often go on holiday to Northumberland and at Alnwick Castle there's a fantastic tree house, with rope bridges and walkways high up in the trees. When I'm walking on that rope bridge, I find myself gripping quite tightly onto the hand ropes and watching my feet every step of the way, making sure they find a plank to step on. The effort of doing this is so much greater than regular walking – if anyone tries to talk to me when I'm on there (even something completely mundane, like, 'What's for tea, Mum?') I find myself saying, 'Don't talk to me now, I'm concentrating on walking', which, even at the time, sounds a bit absurd, but is absolutely how I feel in that moment! Take me off the rope bridge and there's nothing I like more than going for a walk with a friend and chatting away as we walk – because however bumpy or rocky the ground we're walking over, I don't have that same sense of instability or peril that I have on the rope bridge.

HAMRAY: A CHILD'S DESCRIPTION OF GRAVITATIONAL INSECURITY

Hamray is a seven-year-old girl. As part of the assessment of her vestibular system, I asked her if she and her foster carer would come and lie down on the mat, so that we could do the next activity. The little girl immediately stepped back, folding her arms and saying that she was scared to do that. I asked what was scary and she said that she worried she might fall off the edge of the mat. I found that such a great description of how it must feel to have such an underdeveloped gravitational security, and so sobering to think of how hard everyday life must feel for her.

Putting all of these together – the stable base postural control gives us, a horizon that stays still while we're moving and a feeling of stability and connectedness with the ground – we can see why this really is a foundation system. Another reason why we can think of the vestibular system as a foundation system is because of how early in our lives it starts to develop. For a typically developing baby, the vestibular system is fully formed and working by 22 weeks in utero, but the vestibular nuclei actually start working nine weeks after conception (Ayres 2005) as the baby moves in response to the movements of the mother. Like all of our sensory systems, the vestibular system needs movement to feed it, and if you watch footage of babies in utero, you'll see just how much a typically developing baby is moving all through pregnancy. As technology progresses, we can see with increasing clarity the world of the developing infant and there are some great YouTube clips of babies of about 20/22 weeks moving and stretching around in the womb, that are fascinating to watch (try searching '20–22-week-old baby in utero'). As the baby grows and moves in utero, their preferred positions change, and in the last couple of months of pregnancy, when the baby is, to our way of thinking, upside down and moving around, this is like a feast for the vestibular system, really priming it and preparing it for the challenges of the outside world.

Our brain and central nervous system are phenomenally complex and I want to try and get the balance right here, not giving too simplistic or too complex an explanation of the working of this system. I'm just hoping to provide a helpful amount of information and, if you're interested in knowing more, then Ayres' 2005 book, *Sensory Integration and the Child*, would be a good starting point. Or, if you're really wanting to get into the neurophysiology of it all, *Neuroscience: Exploring the Brain* (Bear, Connors and Paradiso 2006) offers clear explanations, pictures and an accompanying website.

The receptors for the vestibular system are in the ears and comprise two structures: otoliths and semi-circular canals. These are tiny structures with hair-like cilia that project from them. There are crystals on these hair-like cells and every time we move our heads, these receptors are stimulated and they send electrical impulses along the vestibular nerve. These two sets of structures are stimulated by different sorts of movement; otoliths detect movement that is in a straight line (forward and back or side to side), while the semi-circular canals detect movement that involves changes of direction. This information joins other electrical information flowing along the vestibular nerve, down the spinal cord and out to the muscles that are involved in keeping us upright – so lengthening our bodies and ensuring good muscle tone (Ayres 2005). All of this fantastically complex process happens unconsciously – we don't have to think about how to maintain an upright posture in relation to the pull of gravity as our vestibular system is just working all the time from that earliest point of conception until our very last moment. When we come on to the proprioceptive system, we'll see that none of these systems work in isolation. The vestibular system and the proprioceptive system are constantly exchanging information – all the time that messages are going out to the muscles, messages are coming back from the muscles and joints, giving feedback about position and movement. It really is amazing.

For our purposes, we need to know that for the vestibular system to develop, it must have stimulation and movement. Without loving, nurturing relationships, babies are not moving as much as their systems need, and so this system is very often underdeveloped in children who have experienced developmental trauma. Babies in utero who have been exposed to drugs or alcohol or whose movement has been depressed because of maternal stress, can be born with a vestibular system that is already much less developed than it should be.

Typically, what we see in children with underdeveloped vestibular systems relates absolutely to the function of the system, so if a well-functioning vestibular system maintains a degree of muscle tone that affords good upright posture, when this system is underdeveloped, muscle tone is usually weak and children can seem quite floppy. Children with underdeveloped vestibular systems can often either tire very easily or never seem to tire.

A well-functioning vestibular system allows us to move freely and easily in our environments, but if a system hasn't had adequate experiences/levels of input, then we may see fearfulness about movement – no sense of connectedness to the ground or feeling of being well balanced. But remember, if children are struggling with something or if they feel themselves to be different from their peers, they'll work hard to find a way round things, to try and compensate for areas of underdevelopment. So a child who feels insecure in their movements may do things very quickly – speed can make up for a huge lack of control – and it is only when we slow them down that we can see whether doing things quickly is a choice or a necessity.

AMBER, SEAN AND ELSA: ASSESSING VESTIBULAR FUNCTIONING
AMBER
I met Amber when she was 14. You can read a much fuller account of our work together in Chapter 17, but for now I want to describe her movement when I met her. I went to the family home and Amber was upstairs when I arrived. She walked down to meet me, gripping onto the banister with both hands, stepping with both feet onto each step, and watching her feet as she walked down. I felt as if I was watching a very old person. When she got to the bottom of the stairs and walked into the living room I could see how stiff and awkward she looked in her movements – so already, within the first minute or two of meeting her, I was beginning to wonder about her vestibular functioning. Why was she holding herself so stiffly? Why couldn't she walk down the stairs without holding on so tightly to the banister?

SEAN
At the other end of the spectrum, but with the same underlying difficulties, was Sean, who was like a rocket in the room where we met, zooming around and doing everything at a million miles an hour (all the time announcing that it was all too easy for him!). His parents and I worked really hard together to keep slowing him down, and we could see, when he was doing things slowly, just how wobbly he was, how many times he fell over and how often he bumped into things. When we'd finished the session and were going back downstairs, Sean went down on his bottom for the first half and then did a huge jump down the second half. This was quite effective, but it was only when I got him to come back up and try to walk down that we could see that speed was making up for a lack of stability – he held on to the banister

with both hands and was really tentative, going very slowly and looking down at his feet as he went.

ELSA
Elsa presented differently again and it was sitting drawing that really exposed the gaps in her vestibular system. She held herself very tightly and sat with her legs crossed – it looked as if she was trying to make her body as small as possible and keep it as close to her core as she could. Unfortunately, even this wasn't enough to compensate for that very unstable core – as she started to draw, she fell off the chair, then when she was back on, she opted to turn the page every time she needed to change direction with her picture, so that she could keep her arm very stiffly by her side and hardly move herself at all.

Indicators that might suggest a child's vestibular system is underdeveloped
Core strength and stability

- Looks quite floppy and seems to have a saggy core and limbs, especially their arms. They might struggle to have straight arms when they are in a crawling position.

- Moves very slowly or stiffly. I find that I need to look more closely at a child who is working very hard to keep themselves upright to really notice what is happening. Sometimes, when a child is holding themselves very stiffly, it is as if they're trying to use their arms like an exoskeleton, and minimizing the movements of their legs. The less bending and changing of direction they have to do, the easier things are.

- Has problems sitting still on a chair/at a table, doing something like eating or writing. As you watch children sitting, try to work out where they get their stability from – is it coming from their core? Are their bodies upright? How do they manage on a stool without a back? What is their head position like? Are they lying across the desk to write? Or do they seem to need to prop their head up with their arms?

Assuming that there aren't other medical explanations for this, these can all be clues that the vestibular system may not be as well developed as they need it to be.

• Always seems to be leaning on something – and if that prop moves, they fall over. I remember walking into a room where a foster carer and her nine-year-old foster child were waiting for me. They were sitting on the sofa and the boy was snuggled up to her. My first thought was how nice that looked, but that changed a bit when the foster carer got up to say hello and the boy just fell into the space she'd been sitting in, and it became clear that he didn't have enough core stability to hold himself up.

Gravitational insecurity

• Seems uncertain about moving – so perhaps is slow or hesitant in movements, or, at the other end of the spectrum, can only do things at top speed.

• Walks along not lifting their feet off the ground, but preferring to slide their feet along the ground if possible.

• Dislikes rapid changes of direction – prefers not to play games like chasing or football.

• Needs to walk down the stairs holding on to the banister (after about the age of four).

• Doesn't like stepping stones or jumping that involves both feet being off the ground at the same time.

• Struggles to gauge depth or negotiate moving objects and is often bumping into things – there is a big difference between children who can kick a football that's moving and children who need themselves and the football to be still to start with.

• Slides along walls as they walk.

A note about normal development: There's a stage in early adolescence, often around the time of a growth spurt, when teenagers become quite gangly and awkward in their movements. Children who previously sat up straight might now slouch across the table as they're eating or slide along walls as they're walking. This is all completely normal and seems to disappear as teenagers get a bit more comfortable with their new body shape and size. It's important not to misinterpret this as an underdeveloped sensory system or an indication of something being wrong – but it does make assessing young people at this stage of development much more challenging and it's important to get a good picture of pre-adolescent movement and development from their carer or parent.

Chapter 10

Assessing the Development of the Vestibular System: Core Strength and Stability

W E'VE been thinking about movement and the clues that we can get about the state of development of the foundation systems from watching a child move and play. In this part of the assessment, I want to understand the stage of development of a child's vestibular system. What's important here is what they can do now and the potential there is for growth and development rather than any age-expected norms. No matter what a child is able to do, I want them to leave the assessment feeling as if it's been good fun and wanting to keep doing more of the games and activities. So even if they can't lift their body off the ground at all in prone extension (see below), I praise their effort and say how fantastic their determination is, and that it's going to help them to get so much better by the next time I see them if they do a little bit of practice every day!

I've found that it's really common for children to have islands of good functioning within these systems and that this isn't necessarily indicative of the functioning of the whole system. Even when I meet young people who may be excelling in a particular field, I try and keep an open mind about the overall development of their system and whether the whole system is working as well as it could be. Generally, when children have islands of good functioning, especially good core stability, it can mean that the other systems will grow more quickly. But don't be fooled; a stable core doesn't mean that everything else will be intact – in fact, it's not even a particularly good predictor of gravitational security! And it's not unusual to find a child who has islands of good core stability but no shoulder girdle strength, but that's all part of what makes it interesting! I'll talk about this more in Chapter 14.

In terms of the process of the assessment, I tend to start with the tactile system and then move on to the vestibular system. I do it this way round because asking children and young people who you've probably only met a minute before to lie on the floor as soon as they come into the room can feel a bit too strange; so doing something first to make them feel more comfortable with you and be in the space can be helpful. Sometimes, if a child is very energetic and bouncing around, and has been primed that we're going to be playing lots of games on the floor, then starting with activities on the floor feels just right and can be quite settling.

One of the things that I hadn't expected, when I started training practitioners in the BUSS model, was how strange and different they might find the idea of moving and being on the floor with the children. Training as an OT, you get very used to physically moving your clients, but for social work, psychology and education colleagues, this was quite a different experience. As you'll see, the model is fairly 'hands on' (if a child is not able to get their body into the right position, I work with parents to help them to do this) and again for some practitioners, this has taken quite a lot of thought and practice. If I'm asking a child or young person to lie on the floor, then I need to be lying on the floor too – it would feel very strange to be sitting in a chair or standing above them. It is much better to 'do with' rather than 'do to' someone.

For this part of the assessment, I use the following materials:

- Table and chairs that are the correct height for the child or young person being assessed.

- Paper and a (sharp) pencil.

- Two climbing ropes (or something similar), each about 1.5 metres in length. They need to be the same dimension; something that's big enough so the child can feel it with their feet but not so big that it's uncomfortable for them to walk on.

- Cushions (x 12) and non-slip mats (x 12). I find it's helpful to have both, because cushions provide a nice landing and are great on carpets, but are too slippy on a wooden or laminate flooring. It's important to be able to discern whether a child is slipping around because they can't balance, or whether they might be moving because they are on a slippy floor!

Assessing the development of the vestibular system. Part 1: Core strength and stability

As I've been training BUSS practitioners, I've noticed that they often go through a process of thinking that some of these activities to assess vestibular functioning sound very straightforward, but when they meet with a child and try to notice all the things that they haven't noticed before, and about how the child is doing the activities, suddenly it feels a lot more complicated. Each child needs a bespoke intervention – I think of it as the 'art' of the intervention.

Sitting at a table and drawing

I sit at the table and ask the child to sit with me and draw the best picture they can of a whole person. I give them a pencil and five or six pieces of paper. There are parts of this assessment that veer into looking at proprioceptive functioning, and we'll come back to this when we think about assessing the development of that system, as well as lots of information about a child's sense of themselves and their confidence in drawing in front of someone, but for now, our focus is on core stability. I need to notice how the child is sitting – where are they getting their stability from? There are lots of things a child might do to try and hold themselves in position if that stability isn't coming from their core. It's helpful to notice the following:

- Are they sitting on their bottom with their feet on the floor (remember that 90 degrees at hips, knees and ankles)?

- Are they leaning against the back of the chair and stretching their legs far out in front of them or are they sitting up with their knees bent?

- Are they sitting with their legs bent up beside them on each side, so if you were to look at them from above it would look like a W shape?

- Are they leaning or lying across the table to draw?

- Do they need to prop their head up with their hands?

- Do they move around a lot?

- Do they fall off the chair?

All of these provide a rich source of information about core strength and stability. You have to be looking at the big picture and not just watching what the child is drawing! We're so used to looking at the picture the child is drawing and thinking about that, whereas here we need to be thinking of the process. How do they approach the task, what's happening on a bodily level? How is the body trying to play to its strengths to do something like drawing or writing, which is pretty tricky for a lot of children? Of course, the pictures themselves also give a great insight into the child's sense of themselves and I'm very interested in how they draw their bodies – and how this compares with the picture they draw at the end of the intervention (you can see Scan and Elsa's pictures in Chapters 15 and 16). For this part of the assessment, it's important to focus on the child's body and how they are doing the drawing.

Lying on the floor in a straight line

For this activity, I ask children to lie down on their tummies, with their arms stretched out in front of them, as if they are Superman, Supergirl, or a swimmer ready to swim over some waves. I lie down beside them and encourage a parent or carer to lie beside them. With younger children, I often ask the parent or carer to lie down first, then see if the child can lie beside them, and I say something like, 'Let's see if you can stretch as far as daddy', so they're not feeling as self-conscious or that it is a pretty weird thing for someone to be asking them to do!

Here I notice the following things:

- The alignment of the child's body – could we draw an imaginary straight line from the top of their head and finish in-between their heels?

- Can they position their arms in a straight line from the shoulders, stretching out on the floor above their head?

- What is the head position like? You might like to try this yourself and notice what you do with your head. Generally, unless your vestibular system is underdeveloped, we make sure that our head is positioned so that we can see what's happening. If a child has an underdeveloped vestibular system, they tend not to do this and their forehead is just on the floor.

If a child's body is not in a straight line, I correct it at this point, making sure that parents or carers know what to do to support their child in getting into this position at home. The correction is usually quite simple, and involves encouraging the child to have their head up so they can see what's happening and then moving their legs to be in a straight line with the rest of their body. Sometimes there are mirrors in the rooms that I use and this can be really useful for older children to be able to check their own position, and to get them in the habit of noticing whether what they're thinking their body is doing and what it's actually doing are the same thing. This can be especially useful when we move on to doing activities that involve more moving.

Prone extension

From that Superman/Supergirl position of arms stretched out in front of their head, I ask the child to see if they can lift their arms and legs up off the floor so that only their tummy is still touching the floor. (I've generally primed parents and carers that this is what we're going to do, so that they know what's coming, because, for  most of us, it's pretty challenging! Make sure you try this yourself – you'll get a good idea of what it feels like.) Generally by the age of eight, typically developing children can get a good 45-degree angle between the floor and their shoulders, with their heads up, and hold this for about ten seconds, with their arms out straight. As we get older, we seem to get less good at this – so don't be surprised when you try it if you struggle to get much elevation, although it's good to notice where you feel it in your body and how challenging (or not) it feels to do. With this activity, it's the extent to which the child is able to control this movement and hold the position that is important.

- How do they do it – does their head come up with their arms?

- Can they get any elevation? How much?

- If they can get some elevation, can they hold that position? How long does it take for them to get tired? What happens when they do? Do they just go back down on the floor or do they roll onto their side?

- Can they keep their arms in a straight line or are they tending to bend, or do they bring them down by their sides? Or are they using their arms to prop themselves up on the floor?

I tend to do this a few times, partly so that the child knows what they're doing and also because I'm keen to see if there's any shift in how they do it as the activity becomes familiar. As you'll know from trying it yourself, it's pretty tiring, so keep noticing how the child is doing and have a break if they need one. If a child isn't able to get any elevation at all, but seems keen to keep trying, then I'll ask their parent or carer to hold on to the child's legs, around the ankles, and act like a lever for them to push against, to see whether this helps them to get started. Again, try this yourself, just tucking your feet under the sofa and trying to pull yourself up from there – it really is much easier! And if we're thinking about those ladders of challenge, you'll already have a good idea of where you might ask children to start doing this activity – prone extension is a great way to build core strength.

I find that asking families to take a photo of the best prone extension position their child is able to get into on the day of the assessment is really helpful for us all in tracking progress.

ELSA, NADIA, SEAN AND AMBER: A FIRST LOOK AT VESTIBULAR FUNCTIONING

ELSA

Sitting drawing – I touched on this briefly in Chapter 9. As we were sitting at the table drawing I could see how unstable Elsa was. She kept moving about in her chair, crossing her legs very tightly and drawing them up towards her body. She was trying to sit very still and looked very stiff – when she wanted to change direction on her picture she moved her piece of paper instead of changing direction with the pencil. She fell off the chair a couple of times during the drawing of the picture. She didn't seem fazed by this and I got the impression that it happened a lot. I asked her how she found writing at school and she said that she found it really hard – she's got good ideas in her head and she knew how she wanted the letters to look, but they didn't come out that way. I noticed that she was pressing down really hard as she drew and I could see the outline of the picture on the sheets of paper that had been underneath.

Her mum mentioned at this point that at home Elsa was always getting up and down from her chair during mealtimes and often fell off her chair at home. They felt unsure about whether this was because Elsa wasn't interested in what she was eating, or if it was because she couldn't really stay focused, so it was interesting to think about what impact building her core stability would have on that. Spoiler alert – I'm pleased to say it helped a lot!

Lying on tummy – Elsa could hold a good straight line on her tummy, with her head looking up. This is always so encouraging

– any island of good functioning is great and gives something to build from.

Prone extension – Elsa tried really hard with this, but even with her dad holding her feet she wasn't able to lift her upper body off the carpet. We talked about how brilliant it was that she knew in her mind exactly what she wanted her body to do, and that if she and dad were to practise every day between now and the next time I saw them, I was positive that she'd be able to do it.

So, from this we could see that, although there are islands of a system that were developing, there was still a lot of work to be done to build Elsa's core stability up to a level that would allow her to feel that her body was working with her, rather than her fighting against it.

NADIA

You might remember Nadia from Chapter 7 on the tactile system. She was six years old when I met her, and at that time she was putting stones into her shoes so that she could feel her feet.

Sitting drawing – Nadia was really wriggly and squirmy on the chair as she was drawing. This is a good example of why it's very important to put the information from all of the parts of the assessment together before making a plan. At first glance, this might have looked like an underdeveloped vestibular system: we needed to gather the information from the rest of the vestibular and proprioceptive parts of the assessment to really understand and make sense of it.

Lying on tummy – Nadia could do this without any difficulty. She got straight into a beautiful straight line!

Prone extension – Nadia made a good attempt at this but was quite wobbly (falling over to the side) and managed about 20 degrees for a couple of seconds. She quite enjoyed the challenge of doing this and kept trying to keep herself in position and get a bit higher. She was delighted when I suggested her parents take a photo and said that if she practised every day for the next three weeks, I thought she would be able to go twice as high and stay up for twice as long!

With Nadia, while there were undoubtedly some islands of good core stability, there were still areas where there was room for growth. It is important to keep remembering that we're looking at underdeveloped systems, so if there are any areas where it looks as if there could be room for improvement, then I always try and go with that. Don't be tempted to compare a child with an underdeveloped system to another child with an underdeveloped system – the bar needs to be much higher. Often parents are surprised when I say that I think we could get their child's systems working so much better, and they say that they thought they were pretty good, because they're better than they used to be. That's completely understandable (and it's always great to hear parents defending their children and correcting me for saying their child isn't doing amazingly well!), but being better at something than they used to be is not the same as being as good as they could be.

SEAN
Sitting drawing – it was a real challenge to get Sean to sit at the table because he wanted to be running and rushing around, showing me all the fantastic flips and tricks that he could do, so we started the assessment with the floor-based activities. When we came back to sitting towards the end of the assessment, I could only persuade him to stay sitting for a very short time, but from what I could see, Sean seemed to balance himself at the table by having both forearms completely on the table and trying to hold his body very stiffly to sit quite still. When he was drawing, it was a whole-body movement; he wasn't able to isolate his fingers or his hand to do this, and his parents and I could see that without enough core stability, he couldn't manage anything that was as far away from his core as writing or drawing.

Lying on tummy – Sean was really up for doing this, and his dad lay down beside him. Sean was busy telling me that this was far too easy for him, but his parents and I could see that he couldn't get his body into a straight line. He could stretch his arms out in front of him, but his forehead was on the floor and then his body just veered off to one side from his shoulders – I think of this as being a bit like a banana back. Because he was quite a long way from straight, I asked his mum to come and lie down with us too, and encouraged them all to lie really close together with Sean in the middle, so that he was like a little hot dog in a roll. At this stage, he really needed that exoskeleton of his parents to keep his body in a straight line.

Prone extension – as you might expect, if a child is really struggling to hold their body in a straight line, you wouldn't normally see any elevation – and even with his dad doing it beside him and his mum holding his feet, Sean couldn't lift his upper body off the floor.

Understanding how weak Sean's core was helped us all to make sense of his rushing around – he really wasn't getting the stability he needed from his core, and so doing everything at top speed probably felt like a good idea! Much better to do it fast and get it over with, than for everyone to be able to see how hard it is to stay upright! I often see this in children and whenever a child tells me that they're really good at doing 'flips' I begin to wonder about core stability. It was a great moment in rebuilding an underdeveloped system of another eight-year-old boy, Kofi, when he told me that he didn't have to do flips at school anymore. He explained that he'd been doing them so that he had some control over when he fell down, otherwise the other children laughed at him for falling down all the time – but now he could stand without falling over and so didn't need the flips anymore!

AMBER

You will remember Amber from Chapter 9. She was 14 when I was working with her.

Sitting drawing – I saw Amber at home and she was very anxious when I met her and seemed tired. We sat on the sofa and my overwhelming impression of her was that she would have liked to have been invisible – she seemed to push herself back against the sofa and not want to be noticed. I was very conscious that Amber had seen so many professionals over the past ten years, all of whom had ideas about what they wanted her to do and who were then disappointed when they saw her again and things were no different. I wanted to start very gently with her, so spent longer than normal sitting on the sofa and chatting about how systems should develop for babies, and watching some YouTube clips of typically developing babies. She seemed to get more animated as we did this, and asked me at one point if that might mean that she didn't have something wrong with her – that she might be someone whose systems were underdeveloped. I said that I certainly hoped so and really wanted to work with her and her mum to go back and fill in the gaps and see how things went.

I didn't want to overwhelm Amber with a whole assessment. I'd got a lot of information from watching her walk down the stairs, but I did ask her to draw me a picture of a person. I could see that it was as laboured as the rest of her movements; she held her body very stiffly and it was a whole-body movement, all the time gripping her pencil so tightly and sometimes gouging through the page as she drew. We talked about how hard school must be – by 14 she was being expected to take down notes quickly, and she talked about not even managing to write in her planner what her homework for that day was before the lesson was over.

Lying on tummy – by the time we'd done the drawing and talked about how hard writing was, Amber was up for us thinking together about her core stability. I talked to her about the idea of her body being like a crane and it made good sense to her. She was happy to try lying in a straight line on her tummy and we could see, when she was on her tummy, that she couldn't get her body into a straight line – very like Sean, she could stretch her arms out in front of her but then the rest of her body just veered off to the side like a banana.

Prone extension – Amber seemed quite happy to keep trying things, so I asked her and her mum to lie on the floor beside each other on their tummies, and tuck their feet under the sofa before trying to lift their arms and torsos off the floor. Both found it really challenging, but Amber seemed pleased by the idea that I thought that she could get a lot better at this if she practised it at least six times a day for the next couple of weeks.

So we can see with Amber that even though she had been living for ten years as part of a loving, nurturing family, those early gaps in her foundation systems hadn't filled themselves in and it was so sad to think of all the ways in which she hadn't been able to progress because of that. Amber's mum talks very movingly about the emotional and psychological impact of this in Chapter 17.

Chapter 11

Assessing the Development of the Vestibular System: Gravitational Security

JUST noticing how a child moves around gives really good information about gravitational security. You might have tried this before, but it is helpful to do it again and think about the part of the action where your feet are off the floor. Walk around and think about how you're moving. Then find some time to watch the child you're thinking about walking and see what you notice.

- Does their walking seem effortless and have a nice fluid quality to it?

- Are their feet coming off the ground?

- Is their foot doing a 'heel strike, toe peel' action (see Chapter 2) when they walk?

- Are they leaning or sliding along walls as they walk?

- Can they turn just their head to look around or do they move their whole body?

- Are they using the wall to support themselves when they're doing something like putting on their shoes?

- Do you notice them propping themselves up when they are standing still – perhaps leaning on something or popping a knee up on a chair?

- Do they fall over a lot?

- Are their parents or teachers describing them as clumsy?

And remember to notice, too, how fast a child is doing things – if everything is done at top speed, just keep slowing things down and notice what happens.

Activities to notice gravitational security

I do three different activities to look at gravitational security, and put this information together with what parents and carers have noticed as well as any other things that I've seen as part of the assessment process. If a child is clearly very unstable – I can usually see this from just watching them walking around – then it's not always necessary to do all three parts of this assessment. I want to make sure that I'm getting enough information, but constantly asking children to do things that they know they can't succeed at can be very discouraging and I definitely want to stop before we get to that point. Unlike the games in the tactile system, here it's obvious to children if they can or can't do the activities. So, as long as I know that I'm going to be seeing the child and their family again, I keep going until I've got enough information to know where I need to start, and I might pick up the bits of the assessment that we haven't done in this first session when we meet again in a month or two.

Activity 1: Walking up and down a flight of stairs

If this is a familiar activity for a child, then you can get lots of information about gravitational security from watching them do this. Only once have I seen a child who had never been on a staircase before, and if that is ever the situation, then just notice what happens as they're going up and down (but I wouldn't attribute too much significance to it, other than how they manage something new). If I see a child in a building that doesn't have stairs, then I ask parents or carers to video their child going up and down the stairs at home and bring that with them to the assessment so that we can watch it together. It's important to check that what I'm seeing is typical – some children freeze right up or become much more exuberant than normal when a camera is produced or someone is watching them. I need to know whether what I'm seeing is what normal looks like for that child.

While it is interesting to notice how a child walks up the stairs (especially if they're leaning forwards so that their hands are on every step before they step onto it), it's really coming down the stairs that yields the most useful information about gravitational security. If you think about the difference between going up and coming down stairs, when you're going up, you can always see the next step in front of you, but coming down, you've got that 'leap of faith' moment when you take your foot off the step you're on and step forwards, not immediately finding something to land on.

Again, it's important to notice what the child's whole body is doing. Just as I talked about with the exercise of the child drawing, we need to look at the whole child and the environment, noticing the process. It's also important to ask parents or carers if the stairs at home are similar or different to these ones – some houses have really steep staircases while others are much easier to navigate. Some families don't like handrails, while others have them on both sides – there's great variety!

Once I've established those things, then it's helpful to watch as the child goes up and comes down the stairs. There are a number of aspects to consider:

- Is their body still? Is their trunk giving a stable base for the work?

- Where are they looking? It's usual for us to watch where we're going but not to have to look at what our feet are doing to get us there.

- Are they holding onto the banister? With one hand? Both hands? Or are they using the wall to steady themselves?

- Do they come down at a normal sort of speed or is it very fast? Or very slow?

- Do they come down on their feet or do they need to be closer to the floor, perhaps coming down on their bottom?

- Does it seem a fluid, confident movement, or do you feel that the child is going to fall at any moment?

And one last thing about this activity – I never tell a child how I want them to do this, because I'm interested in seeing how they do it. So I don't prompt by asking the child to come down without holding on, or looking at me – all of that can come later. At this stage, we really just want to notice how they do it, and see if that gives us useful information about the development of their vestibular system. As we'll come back to in Chapter 13, this activity also provides a lot of information about the proprioceptive system, but for now, we'll just focus on the gravitational security arm of the vestibular system.

And finally, if I ask the child to try anything different when they're coming down a flight of stairs, I make sure that I'm standing at the bottom of the staircase and ask them to only go up five steps before they come down again. I need to feel confident that I could catch them if asking them to do it differently is very difficult and they get wobbly or unstable. I often ask children to show me how they normally come down a few times, and then I might ask them to do it again, this time, for example, coming down the last five steps without holding on to the banister – or, if they've been holding on with two hands, only holding on with one hand. I'm looking to see what their body does when I make this change – do they become stiff? Wobbly? Do they fall?

Activity 2: Tightrope walking

We'll come back to this activity when we're thinking about the proprioceptive system because, as you'll be getting the hang of by now, our bodies need both systems to be working well to perform these tasks. But while I'm trying to help you to get better at noticing the difference in how they work, we'll stick with what we can learn about vestibular functioning from this activity. So to start with, I use the two climbing ropes and put them down on the floor in two straight lines, parallel and so that they are hip-distance apart for the child. I ask parents or carers to stand on the ends so that the rope is taut – it's much harder to do it on a wriggly rope. I ask children to take their shoes off so that they can really feel the rope with their feet. First, I show the child what I want them to do – to walk along the rope from one end to the other. I stand tall as I'm doing this, and put my arms out to the side so I look like a professional tightrope walker. With younger children, I often pretend that we're explorers, out in the Amazon and crossing over a river or walking from tree top to tree top, just to make it more fun. I then ask the child to do the same. I ask them to do this five or six times so that there are lots of chances to notice how they do it. And just as I talked about with the stairs, I don't prompt about how they should do it, I just want to notice how they manage it.

As I'm observing a child doing this, I think of that game Misfits that I mentioned at the beginning of the book, and I divide their body into head, body and legs, seeing what each part is doing and then seeing how it is working as one unit:

- Where are they looking? As I said with the stairs, it's usual to look at where we're going but not to have to watch every step. What is their trunk doing? We want a nice stable core, so not much wobbling around or swaying from side to side.

- Is there a fluidity to the movement? We want stability but not rigidity or stiffness.

- Are their feet on the rope? Both of them? Each time? Are they lifting their feet up and placing one foot in front of the other each time? Left foot in front, then right foot? Or are they keeping their feet side by side? Or is only one foot leading?

- Are they lifting their feet up and placing one foot in front of the other each time – left foot in front, then right foot? Or are they keeping their feet side by side?

- How fast are they going? Remember the idea of speed making up for a lack of control. I keep slowing things down until I've got a good picture of what's happening on a bodily level.

Here I want to take us back to that idea of grading an activity. If a child is able to do this well – so walking along the ropes with their feet on the ropes, lifting their feet up and not wobbling around – I need to make it harder; if they're not doing it well, I need to try and break it down further so that I can work out what is making it challenging for them.

Making this activity harder

I show the child how to walk backwards along the tightropes and ask them to have a try. (If we've been pretending to be explorers in the Amazon, I suggest that we keep a very good lookout for jaguars or a poison dart frog…or if they are worried by the thought of being pursued by a jaguar or poison dart frog, we might pretend to be explorers looking for a beautiful and rare bird, and we might have heard something that makes us think it's quite close by, so we need to keep looking forwards as we walk backwards towards our camp…). Here, I want to see if the child is able to maintain balance without using their eyes, and also (veering into proprioceptive functioning) if they're able to feel for the rope with their feet.

I often suggest a child tries going backwards, even if they've been a little bit wobbly going forwards. That's because sometimes if a child is feeling very self-conscious and anxious, they can be wobbly walking forwards but actually really good walking backwards, which suggests that the wobbling was more about them feeling nervous and self-conscious than necessarily about core stability or gravitational security. But I wouldn't suggest it if the child was completely falling off the ropes or their feet hadn't even touched the ropes.

From here I move the child on to one rope and repeat the same sequence of going forwards and then going backwards, noticing all of the same things. If there is a big difference in how wobbly the child becomes on one rope from when they were on two, then it's clear that the child needs to spend longer on two ropes before moving on to one. If they can manage one rope well, but there are islands of instability in this system, then there are lots of ways to make it harder, which we will come on to when we think about how to rebuild an underdeveloped system.

Making this activity easier

How I grade this depends on what I've noticed about how the child is doing it. Perhaps the most common thing to see, apart from wobbling, is children who watch their feet every step of the way. With these children, I'm interested in what happens if they're not watching their feet – because this helps me to discern whether there are gaps in the vestibular or proprioceptive systems. So I might ask them to look up at their dad as they're walking along (or whoever is standing at the other end of the rope) and tell me what colour his eyes are or how many buttons on his shirt. It really doesn't matter what it is – it's about raising their eye line and us noticing, for this part of the assessment, if this makes them more wobbly or not.

If, as soon as the child takes their eyes off what they're doing, they become very wobbly, then that's an indicator to me that there's some work to be done on the vestibular system, both in terms of core stability and gravitational security. We'll revisit this when we come on to the proprioceptive system, because sometimes children are watching their feet because they're not getting the messages from muscles and joints about body position.

Noticing the subtleties of how a child is moving takes a lot of time and practice. When I'm training practitioners, we spend a lot of time looking at children and at videos parents and carers have taken of their children moving, until they're confident about what it is they're seeing. Like any new skill, it all takes time.

If raising a child's eye line has made them more wobbly, this is probably where I want them to start to rebuild that system – but their body needs more help. Again, it is that idea of an exoskeleton – providing stability from outside until they develop it from within. I encourage parents and carers to put their hands on the child's hips and walk beside them as they're doing this, just helping with that core stability. This often feels strange to people – we're used to helping children balance by offering to hold their hand, but if a child is really wobbly then it's more effective to rebuild from the core out. I want the child to experience that sensation of being nice and stable in their trunk and gradually move on from there, so a big part of my task in the assessment session is making sure that the parents or carers are correctly supporting the child.

If a child is so wobbly that they're falling off the rope, then I don't go any further with this part of the assessment. That's enough information to know that there is work to be done, and that I need to go back to simpler vestibular activities to build the gaps in the systems before we return to this one.

I sometimes use this activity when I'm training and it's really helpful if people are able to think about what it's like to be asked to walk along a rope. On a recent training with colleagues I work with and know quite well, I was interested to hear one person talk about how nerve racking it was and how worried she was that she wouldn't be able to do it. She said that she had to do some serious self-talk – come on, it's only walking, you know how to walk, you can do this! But if that's how a group of adults with well-functioning systems feel, imagine how it might feel for children who crash and bang around and never seem to land things right. It's so important to be constantly working with parents and carers in creating an environment for the assessment which is as facilitating and encouraging as it possibly can be.

Activity 3: Jumping from cushion to cushion

This is another activity that gives great information about how a child manages when their feet are off the floor, and how their body copes with the demands of such an activity. To assess how a child is managing this, I find it useful to do that same activity of dividing their body into head, body and legs, and using roughly the same criteria as I talked about for tightrope walking, noticing how each part is working on its own and in relation to the rest of the body. If it's clear, from the parts of the assessment that have already been completed, that a child is very wobbly or crashing and banging around everywhere, then I don't do this activity. To jump from cushion to cushion in a controlled way requires some good core stability and if a child has already struggled to go down a flight of stairs and tightrope walk, then it's not necessary to do anything else.

If the child has been able to manage the first two activities then this is a helpful one to do and can add useful information to the bigger picture of how this system is developing.

Assuming I'm on a carpet, I put six cushions down in a line on the floor, with just a small gap in between. I show the child what I want them to do – to jump with their feet together from cushion to cushion, pausing for a moment on each one. Unlike the other activities in this section where we want to see how the child does it without any prompting, for this activity I give very clear instructions about how I want the child to do it, emphasizing the feet together part of the action. I sometimes use some imaginary glue on myself at this stage, gluing my feet together – and I am clear that I want them to try and pause on each cushion before going on to the next one.

(If we've been trekking through the Amazon on the last activity, this might be the part of the adventure where we're trying to cross a river and, depending on the child, you might want to try and land on the 'rocks' so as not to get eaten by the alligators...)

Again, I do this a few times so that there are plenty of opportunities to observe the child.

- What is the child's head doing? Is it fairly still? Where is the child looking?

- Does it look as if they're leading with their head and that their body is in a nice straight line from there, or is it a more jumbled sort of movement?

- What is their trunk doing? We want a nice stable core, so not much wobbling around or swaying from side to side.

- Is there a fluidity to the movement? We want stability but not rigidity or stiffness.

- Do they take off from two feet and land on two feet?

- Is it a staggered landing, with one foot landing before the other?

- Are they landing on the cushion? Near the cushion?

- How fast are they going? Remember the idea of speed making up for a lack of control and that the best information comes from watching a child do things slowly.

If a child isn't able to do this in a controlled way, I don't go any further with this part of the assessment – I just stick with the idea that I've got enough information to know that it would be helpful to do some work on this part of the vestibular system.

To make this activity harder

If a child can manage this without difficulty, it's fun to make things harder and really challenge them! I always enjoy it if we can move on from here, because again it means we've got an island of really good functioning.

Just as I did with the tightrope, I ask the child if they want to try going backwards – and again notice what happens in terms of balance and control of the movement. If there's good control, then I tend to put another row of cushions alongside the first one, so that I can introduce changes of direction, and at this stage we usually play 'Follow My Leader'. I might jump forwards for two cushions, then diagonally, then back, then zig zag to the end of the line. I then suggest to the child that they be the leader so I can see what's happening! If I'm struggling to really make sense of what's going on (and this can be especially tricky if the child is going really quickly), then I ask a parent to be part of the game so that I can 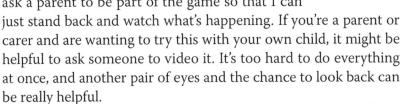 just stand back and watch what's happening. If you're a parent or carer and are wanting to try this with your own child, it might be helpful to ask someone to video it. It's too hard to do everything at once, and another pair of eyes and the chance to look back can be really helpful.

With this, I'm still holding in mind all of the points we discussed for tightrope walking, but I also want to notice what happens to the child's trunk. Can they maintain a strong, upright position, so that their body is in a straight line as they're jumping, or, does it look more like their feet leading and their body following – legs, then trunk, then head?

If they're really good at this, we might rearrange the cushions so we've got three rows and do forwards, backwards and sideways. At this stage, if a child is able to do this, I'm thinking that the gravitational security arm of their vestibular system is in pretty fantastic shape!

I just keep going with this until I feel as if we've reached the limit of what a child is able to do but before they start to really struggle.

By this stage of the assessment, I should have good information about core stability and gravitational security.

ELSA, NADIA, SEAN AND AMBER: ASSESSING GRAVITATIONAL SECURITY

ELSA

Walking down a flight of stairs – the first time Elsa went down the stairs she had one hand on the banister and one hand on the wall. She watched her feet with every step, walking down quite slowly, and putting one foot on each step.

When she'd done this a few times, I asked her to go back up five steps from where I was standing at the bottom, and this time to try coming down but just holding on to the banister and not the wall – she did this, watching her feet all the time. After a few repetitions, she was pretty steady doing this and felt a bit more confident.

I asked Elsa to go back up those five steps and for us to do an experiment and to see what happens if she were to try coming down without holding on at all – this time Elsa became really wobbly and only managed a couple of steps before I caught her. We agreed that our experiment had shown us that we needed to get her core much stronger!

Tightrope walking – Elsa tiptoe walked along the two ropes and was quite wobbly. She was actually better going backwards so we tried with one rope and it was interesting to see that she wasn't any more wobbly. We agreed it would be helpful to practise doing this and I talked to her parents about us needing to emphasize the heel strike/toe peel action that we were looking for. This seemed to be a bit of a novelty for Elsa and she appeared to quite enjoy the sensation of using her whole foot in the movement.

Jumping from cushion to cushion – Elsa did this really fast and when I asked her to slow down it was clear that she didn't really have any control of where she was going or how fast she was doing it – she fell off the cushions or landed between them. I didn't go any further with this.

When I put this information together with the assessment of core strength and stability, for Elsa, it was clear that there were significant gaps in core stability and gravitational security and I was keen to get started rebuilding them!

NADIA

Walking down a flight of stairs – Nadia was quite hesitant coming down the stairs, holding on to the banister and watching her feet with every step. She wasn't keen to try coming down without holding on and I didn't push it. The fact that she felt too nervous to try it, especially when I'd seen how confident she was on the other activities, already told me that we needed to work on gravitational security.

Tightrope walking – Nadia was quite stable and confident on two ropes and enjoyed going forwards and backwards. When we changed to only having one rope, Nadia looked much less stable, sliding her feet along the rope rather than lifting them off, and all the time watching her feet. This helpfully added to the picture of gravitational insecurity, with some islands of core stability.

Jumping from cushion to cushion – Nadia looked very similar to Elsa in this, a bit less wobbly, but still struggling to have much control over where she was landing or how far she was jumping.

SEAN

Walking down a flight of stairs – Sean was very tentative about this, wanting to show me how he could jump down. He came down the first half on his bottom but was happy to try walking down the last five steps (within catching distance!). He was very shaky as he walked down, holding on to the banister and watching his feet. He didn't want to try doing this again.

Tightrope walking – Sean slid his feet along the two ropes. I tried putting his shoes on to see if he might be able to step over them, but he just stepped on top of them. Putting this together with Sean walking down the stairs, we could see that as well as a weak core, the gravitational security arm of Sean's vestibular system was also very underdeveloped.

Jumping from cushion to cushion – Sean was very keen to show me how fast he could do this and I struggled to slow him down. But even speed didn't make up for the lack of control – he didn't land on the cushions and usually landed on his knees rather than his feet. We probably didn't need to do this activity; I already had a lot of information that suggested a very underdeveloped system, but because Sean was doing everything so fast, I just wanted to be sure about what I was seeing!

AMBER

I've already described Amber walking down the stairs and so I won't repeat it here – she was very tentative and wobbly, needing lots of scaffolding from the banister and wall.

Tightrope walking – two ropes. Amber slid her feet along the rope and watched her feet all the time. Because I'd already seen how weak her core stability was and thought that we'd build that first, I didn't do any more of this part of the assessment at this stage. I knew that she wouldn't be able to do it and didn't want to do any more things that highlighted the deficiencies in her systems – we'd done enough!

Instead of moving on to look at how the BUSS model starts with rebuilding an underdeveloped vestibular system, I'd like us to think first about the proprioceptive system. They are so intertwined that's it's helpful to understand both before we move on to thinking about rebuilding them.

Chapter 12

The Proprioceptive System

WITH a well-functioning vestibular system providing a good foundation for movement in terms of core stability and gravitational security, the next step is to think now about the quality of that movement and how babies and young children move from those first, staggering steps, to running, skipping, hopping and jumping in a relatively short time. When we're thinking about movement, we need to have an idea of what good movement looks like and to do this it's often useful to watch an athlete at the peak of their performance and really analyze what's happening on a bodily level. Watching someone like Usain Bolt run the 100 metres, we can marvel in the precision, the power, the fluidity of his movement – every part of his body is working efficiently and effectively towards that finish line. No part is moving that needs to be still; there's no unnecessary expenditure of energy; the synchronicity of the action is awe-inspiring. Now, I'm not about to suggest that we can help all of our children run like Usain Bolt (wouldn't that be amazing?), but watching someone at the top of their performance like that helps us to pinpoint what fluid, well-coordinated movement looks like.

If you read traditional sensory integration books (e.g. Kranowitz 2005), the tactile system and the proprioceptive system are often talked about together, and called the 'somatosensory system'. This is partly because of the neurology of it, but when we're thinking about children whose systems are underdeveloped, it is more helpful to know how each system develops, even if there is a lot of overlap in terms of the neural pathways, because we need to maximize the functioning of each part of the individual systems.

As we are people with well-functioning proprioceptive systems, that sense of being comfortable in our own bodies on a physiological level is something we take for granted. Because so much of this happens without us having to consciously think about it, it is easy not to notice it until something goes wrong. When I'm doing training and am trying to help people to notice on a conscious level what is normally an unconscious process, I ask them to close their eyes, and to keep them closed while they reach down and get their drink from under their chairs and take it up to their mouths as if they're going to drink from it. And everyone is always able to do this – we don't need our eyes to show us where our cup is – our brain has already mapped that out earlier, when we were picking our cup up and putting it down. We don't have to think consciously about which part of our body we'll use to pick up the cup; how far to lean forward so as not to over-balance; how much pressure or force to use when we're picking up the cup. No one has ever (yet!) thrown their drink over their shoulder and onto the people in the row behind them – our brain and central nervous system manage all of this on a unconscious level and when it works, we don't even register it on a conscious level.

But it's worth pausing and imagining for a moment what life might feel like if our systems weren't like that. If we had to approach every task by initiating a scan of the area, a motor plan of how we were going to get from A to Z, and how we were going to execute the movement we were going to Z to do – life would feel completely different. Imagine leaning forwards to pick your cup up off the floor and not reliably knowing that you won't topple right off your chair. You can sometimes get a bit of insight into what an underdeveloped proprioceptive system might feel like when you're injured and having to think carefully about the least painful way to do each movement. (I'm currently nursing a couple of cracked ribs, so this is quite close to my heart – who knew hanging out the washing could be such a tricky process!) But even then, we're doing it from a position of having known what good movement feels like. I can't imagine how it feels for children who have never had that feeling of knowing their bodies from the inside working with them in a helpful way. It must be exhausting just trying to get through a day.

There are some hallmarks of what *good proprioceptive functioning* should look like:

- Children get the messages about where their body is from their muscles and joints – and do not have to use their eyes to track their movement.

- Movement is smooth and well coordinated; there's a fluidity and control to it – at the beginning, through the movement and when the movement ends.

- Both sides of the body are working together in a helpful way (bilateral integration and sequencing).

- Upper body and legs are working together so that the body functions as a single, synchronized unit.

These last two points are particularly important for children whose systems are underdeveloped. I think that's because their development has had to adapt to their environment rather than proceeding the way it should have. You'll remember, from Chapter 3, that typically developing children get control of their bodies from the top down (head, neck shoulder girdle and trunk) and from close to the body (proximal) to further away (fine motor control). But for children who have experienced developmental trauma, this is all turned upside down, and they tend to develop from the feet up. It seems to me that, no matter how terrible a child's early experiences are, they will, at some point, get up and walk. For some children, this will be a quite precocious thing – something about how tensely they've been holding themselves, and how being upright feels much safer than being on the floor, means that they walk without any of the foundations of core stability or gravitational security. At the other extreme, we see those children who have done almost no moving at all in those first months, and are still, as late as nine or ten months, as floppy as a newborn baby. All of these children will stand and walk – some much too early, others very late, but they will all have in common the fact that they're doing it without the foundation that those early movement experiences give them: a stable core; gravitational security; a sense of where their body is from the inside; and a body that knows how much pressure or force to use in a movement.

Growing into ourselves on a bodily level

Let's think first about the function of the proprioceptive system in terms of knowing, from the inside, where our body is, before we even start thinking about moving. We build, through experiences of being held and from having the space to play and explore, an internal map of our bodies. So if you were to close your eyes now, you'd know where your toes are, or your knees or elbows, because you'd be able to sense and feel where they are. And we can do that because of all those repeated touch and movement experiences we had as a baby and young child that built the internal map, or precept (Ayres 2005) of our bodies. On a technical level, movement allows our brain and central nervous system to get feedback from receptors in our muscles and joints – the muscle spindles (which detect changes in muscles' length when we're still and when we're moving) and the golgi tendon organs (which give information about the stress and force at a joint). Together all of this contributes to our bodies having a sense of ourselves from the inside.

Sometimes we can catch a glimpse of this happening, for example that moment when a baby finds their feet for the first time. We can see the excitement and delight they have with themselves at how clever they are to have discovered them. It's no coincidence that all this happens before we have language – we grow into ourselves on a bodily level a long time before we are thinking and reasoning about what we're experiencing. How ridiculous it would be for a grown up to say to that baby, 'How does it feel to have found your feet?' We just marvel in the moment and share the wonder of it with the baby.

So all of the movements that babies do in those early days, weeks and months, when they're surrounded by loving relationships, are the beginnings of them knowing their body from the inside out. The more sensorimotor experiences a baby can have, the greater the resource we give babies on a bodily level. It's a bit like building a map of ourselves and our bodies. Really, we want a high level of detail in our map, showing us all sorts of interesting things around and about. If you think of those maps you get of a city that only show the main roads, it's hard to make interesting, off-the-beaten-track excursions to little-known places (and then to find your way back again!). A map with lots of detail gives us lots of choice, and this is what we want for children in terms of them having confidence in their bodies and how they're moving. The greater the range of movement and tactile experiences a baby has, the greater the detail on their bodily map.

This well-detailed body map builds the perfect platform for more complex movement, where the child is standing and beginning that tricky task of negotiating their way through a world of moving and still objects – and that's before we think about fine motor skills! But let's just think for a moment about how this all happens, and how the child moves from lying on their back to being up and about. To understand how this happens, we need to understand a bit about centrally programmed movement.

Centrally programmed movement

As we think about children developing increasingly complex motor skills, it's helpful to differentiate between innate patterns of movement and things that we need to practise to get good at them. Ayres (2005) talks about the idea of 'central programming'. As we've discussed, we're born with lots of reflexes and we don't have to teach babies how to crawl or walk; we just create the right sort of environments and their bodies will assume the correct positions and go through the right sequence of movements. However, it's important to understand the interaction between innate potential and the influence of the environment here.

Although we are born with these phenomenal movements and reflexes already programmed into our brains and central nervous systems, they can't and won't develop without the right environment, by which I mean the loving, nurturing relationships that allow babies to move from highly defensive functioning to being able to 'be' in the moment of an experience, knowing that a loved and trusted adult will take care of them. It's a bit like having a packet of seeds. I was given some beautiful sunflower seeds the other day, but as things stand, they're sitting on the kitchen worktop. Now I hope those seeds are going to grow into beautiful tall sunflowers, but none of that is going to happen unless I plant them and then take good care of them. Just looking at the packet and imagining how lovely they'll look in the garden isn't enough

– and it's exactly the same with babies and learning how to move. The central movement programme is there, but it doesn't happen without them having the chance to practise – and, as we know, babies only move within relationships in which they feel safe and happy. So you can see how interlinked it all is!

PROTECTIVE EXTENSION

Let's think for a moment about this innate capacity and consider one reflex that's helpful in that first year of life: *protective extension*, which I mentioned briefly in Chapter 3. We know that by about six to eight months of age, babies who are spending lots of time sitting unsupported on the floor on their bottoms, in a stimulating environment where they're feeling safe and happy, will begin to try and reach for toys or things of interest around them. What we'll see, as they reach for something, is that tipping point, the point at which they might be going to topple over, and it's at this point that the protective extension reflex leaps into action. The arm on that side will extend and they'll put their hand down on the floor beside them, so that they 'catch' themselves. This protective extension reflex works on either side or if the baby is leaning too far forwards. It is innate, it was there right from birth, primed and waiting for the right stage of development – and all we need to do for it to happen as it's programmed is to create an environment in which the baby is able, on an emotional and a physical level, to explore.

This reflex is helpful not only at this stage of development in encouraging the baby to be bolder in their exploration by protecting them from getting hurt as part of that, but also by paving the way for the next stage of development, where the baby will be supporting themselves on their hands and knees, the beginnings of locomotion. But if a baby never sits unsupported or there is nothing stimulating or interesting around them, or they never feel safe and happy, this just won't happen. And then, what we often see as these children get older, is when they trip or fall, they don't put their arms out to protect themselves, so they fall like trees, flat on their faces.

So, while we're born with the most amazing innate abilities, we need to be able to move and play and to practise enough to get to the point of having lovely smooth, well-coordinated movement. I'm not saying that babies should never sit supported – of course they can (but to be honest, my heart does sink a bit when I go to a house and meet a baby who is sitting in one of those moulded seats that holds their body in a sitting position) – but we need to make sure that it's not all they do. The more chances babies have to move and explore their environment, the bigger the range of movement experiences they will have in their cerebellum – the part of the brain where these movement programmes are stored.

Movement that requires conscious attention

Let's look now about movement that is more like a skill and which we acquire through practice. Ayres (2005) calls this 'motor planning.' These kinds of movements require our conscious attention until we've learned them, and then we can usually do them without thinking too much about it. This includes things like a baby picking up a spoon for the first time, learning to ride a scooter, learning to get dressed, to tie shoelaces, and to write. All of these things require attention and planning to learn how to do them, but where there is a good foundation of vestibular and proprioceptive functioning, then once we've learned and practised them, we don't need to think about them as much. So you can probably write or tie your laces with your eyes closed, or while you're also talking to someone or thinking about something else that's completely unrelated to the task. They quickly form part of that repertoire or map of movement patterns that are stored in the brain and retrieved as needed, often without much conscious thought. We can think of what we'd like to do, such as climb a stile, and the brain and central nervous system are able to send the right messages to our muscles and joints to make it happen, either because we've done it many times before, or because it's similar to something else that is a familiar movement – in this case like stepping over something, or climbing stairs. Because there's already a good repertoire of movement programmes in there, the brain is fairly easily able to take known patterns of movement and adapt them to new situations. But just like Elsa's description of her desire to have nice handwriting, willing the movement isn't enough. Think of that body map – without all those early touch and movement experiences within the context of a loving relationship, Elsa's body map just doesn't have the level of detail in it that could allow her body to carry out this request. Unless the body has good foundation systems and lots of lovely sensorimotor experiences to draw on, it can't execute the movement.

It surprises (and alarms) me at what a young age children with underdeveloped systems become aware of what they can't get their bodies to do, and how this makes them feel different from their peers. As you'll read in the description from Amber's mum in Chapter 17, even in her reception class, Amber was moving herself to sit away from her peers so that they wouldn't be able to see that she couldn't do the writing. And imagine how frustrating it must have been for Elsa (and so many other children I've met) to know exactly what she wanted her body to do, but not be able to get it to do that. As I grew up in Scotland, the tale of Robert the Bruce watching the spider in the cave and being impressed by the way it just kept trying was a fairly constant feature of my primary education. But really, that spider had nothing on the children I meet whose systems are underdeveloped and who just keep going, desperately trying to get it right and to look the same as everyone else.

So, when we're thinking about an underdeveloped proprioceptive system, we need to hold on to the idea of central programming as well as the element of practice that's required to really nail a pattern of movement. A lot of children who are growing up in adversity miss both; they're not going through the stages of development at the right time, so are not having the help of those primitive and protective reflexes to gently move them towards the next stage of development, and are left without the chance to practise those important skills like creeping and crawling.

This is especially important when we think about the idea of our body working as an integrated, synchronized unit. Because that's something that just 'happens' if we go through the normal sequence of experiences at the right stage of development, it's not something we ever have to think about. This can make it harder to work out how to help children who are really out of synch with themselves. The way that our arms swing helpfully as we walk isn't something we've ever had to learn or think about – we can do it because we had good formative movement experiences that have allowed our bodies to develop the way they're designed to. But this is another thing that doesn't happen without those foundation systems being in place, which is why we need to understand the sequence of development so that, when we notice that something is missing (like arms being a helpful part of jumping or running) we can think when it should have come online and go back and fill in the gaps. In this case, the baby really starts to develop their upper body when they're on their tummy, and as they move from here to creeping and crawling. So that's where we need to go back to thinking of lots of games and activities that will make it fun and engaging for the child to be on their tummy and moving around from there.

LITTLE PICTURE/BIG PICTURE

To rebuild these foundation systems, we need to go back and follow the sequence of typical development. This means going back to what we know of how children develop control, from the head down, and from the core out. This is why we need to take children back to being on their tummies on the floor, building shoulder strength and involvement in the movement from there – always holding on to the idea that what we're trying to do is to rebuild an underdeveloped system. It can be very tempting for parents or carers to notice something like arms not swinging as part of the walking movement, and to want to 'add it' to the movement – perhaps getting their child to practise marching, really emphasizing the arms. This isn't helpful because it is reinforcing that upside-down development – from the feet up. All the time we need to go back to the blueprint of typical development and work from that.

It's important not to try to patch up an underdeveloped system, because the child won't be able to generalize the learning. It's much better to go back and fill in the gaps in the foundation systems so that the child can not only learn to swing their arms as a helpful part of the movement, but also have enough core and shoulder strength to be able to skip, run, hurdle, swim, write and use cutlery. So while it's helpful to look at the little picture and hone in on the specifics of movement to see where the difficulties lie, the solution is then to go back to the big picture and see where that would fit in terms of typical development, and start rebuilding from there.

When we think about the other part of well-synchronized movement – the right and left sides of the body working well together – it's helpful to know a bit about the physiology of our brain. The brain is made up of a right and left hemisphere, connected by the corpus callosum, which is like a bridge, consisting of millions of axons (Bear *et al.* 2006). This bridge is what allows us to use both sides of our brains in a connected way, which is phenomenally important in so many things, like movement, language and learning. But, just like all of the other aspects of brain and central nervous system development that we've thought about, the baby needs lots of early movement experiences that involve them crossing the midline of their body and then using both sides of their body together, to develop this bilateral integration and sequencing.

When I'm training practitioners in the BUSS model, I encourage them to watch how children play or organize themselves and their work space – noticing whether they're using both sides of their body together, using all of the space in front of them, or whether they're tending to favour one side or the other. It's usual to favour one side of our bodies (we're fairly familiar with the idea of a dominant hand) but the non-dominant hand usually plays a role in the movement too.

SAMI AND ROSIE: NOTICING HOW A CHILD IS MOVING RATHER THAN WHAT THEY'RE DOING
SAMI
I met Sami, a three-year-old boy. His adoptive parents were concerned that he might be on the autism spectrum, because

there was something quite odd about the way he moved and played. I visited the family at home and when I arrived Sami was playing with a train. I chatted to his parents for a while and noticed that he played the same thing all the time that we were talking. What he was doing was starting at one end of the bay window ledge and pushing his train to the other end, using the arm that was on the same side as the window. He'd then turn around, swap hands, so that he was still using the arm that was on the same side as the window, and go back again. I could see how this might be construed as repetitive and not really being part of a game that developed into something, in the way that you might want it to. But rather than thinking about a lack of imagination or creativity, as you might if you were considering autism, I was curious about why he was turning his whole body to move the train back to the other end of the window ledge, and not just continuing with the same hand, crossing his arm in front of his body to keep playing, or swapping the train from one hand to the other.

I suggested we sit on the floor and play a bit more with the train and some other cars that he had. What we saw on the floor was part of the same picture – either Sami's right hand was playing with the train, zooming it up and down on the right side of his body, or his left hand was playing with a car on the left-hand side of his body. Seeing him do the same thing in two different situations was helpful in building a picture of what might be going on, and I began to ask his parents if he did much passing from one hand to the other when he was playing with his toys. This wasn't something his parents had thought much about. (This is completely normal, as we get very used to our children just doing what they do, and it's often only when someone asks something like this and we stand back and think about it, that we begin to notice patterns.) As they thought about it, they realized that he only ever ate with one hand – he still used his fingers but he never used both hands.

I find that it's most helpful to build up a picture of things like this, otherwise it's very easy to fall into the trap of thinking something is hugely significant when in fact it's an anomaly. Putting those observations along with parents' and carers' expert knowledge of their child allows us to think together about what we're seeing.

ROSIE

In older children, it can be helpful just to observe the way they approach a task. Rosie is an 11-year-old girl I saw recently, and it was as we were doing the feely bag game at the beginning of the assessment that I noticed her left arm was not only lying on her knee all the time, but she was holding it so that it lay a bit behind her body. The way Rosie's non-dominant arm and hand were so far out of things looked quite odd and reminded me of people I've worked with who have had strokes and were neglecting one side of their body. Rosie was really good at finding things in the feely bag with her dominant hand, but when I asked her to try and find things with her non-dominant hand, she really struggled. When we came to do the roller ball game, it was the same picture – her dominant hand could guess straightaway which finger I was rolling the ball up, but she didn't get any of the answers right on her non-dominant hand. You can probably guess which hand I was wanting her to practise playing the feely bag game with...

Underdeveloped proprioceptive systems

If we think about what an underdeveloped proprioceptive system looks like, we tend to see the following characteristics:

- *Movement that is poorly modulated* – usually a mixture of too floppy or too jerky. I sometimes think that it is as if these children flop into the movement and then jerk themselves out of it, with none of the control or coordination to take them from the beginning to the end of a movement that would give it a lovely smooth quality.

- *Children needing to use their eyes or the environment to plan and execute movement,* rather than this information coming from inside their body. For some children, this means watching their feet when they walk or cycle. I met one teenager whose foster carer described him constantly cycling into the oncoming traffic. She wondered if this was a reflection of his mental state and if she ought to be thinking about psychological therapies. We agreed that could be helpful, but that it might be worth just having a think about things from the perspective of an underdeveloped system first. It was only when I saw him come down some stairs, watching his feet every step of the way, and saw his reaction to my request to look at me as he was coming down ('Are you having a laugh? How will I know where my feet are if I can't see them?') that we realized he was cycling into traffic because he had to constantly be watching his feet to pedal. Working with them to know where his body was from the inside rather than having to use his eyes made the world of difference to his cycling – and his carer's stress levels.

- *Lots of crashing and banging* into things or people, perhaps walking over other children at school rather than negotiating their way around them. This is often construed as the child being aggressive, but if they have experienced developmental trauma, I'd always suggest thinking about whether it might be part of an underdeveloped system – banging into something is another way of finding out where your body is if you're not getting those messages from the muscles and joints inside your body.

DAILY CHALLENGES

Imagine what something like carpet time at school feels like for these children – how can you possibly sit up, in a relatively small space, be still and concentrate on what's being said, if you have no sense of where your body is or how to keep it in one place? What we often notice is these children trying to find a solution for themselves, perhaps sliding back from the carpet, trying to find a hard surface to lean against, or some way to orientate themselves. Usually, if the teacher spots them doing this, they redirect them to the carpet to come and sit 'nicely', without any idea that for them this is practically impossible. I'm absolutely not blaming teachers here; in fact, I've yet to meet a teacher who, once they realized that the child was doing this because their foundation system was underdeveloped, wasn't keen to be part of the solution to this. In the short term, this is often encouraging *everyone* to lie on their tummy on the carpet rather than sit on their bottom. This usually requires a bit of rearranging of the space in the classroom, but for children who aren't getting those messages about where their body is from inside, then lying on their tummy gives them lots of feedback about where they are and usually allows them to be part of the lesson, listening to what's happening, rather than their mind being taken up with desperately trying to find something, or someone, to lean on.

I met a parent who was completely exasperated that her five-year-old adopted child bumped into the door frame every time he went from the living room to the kitchen. 'How can he not know where the door frame is?' she asked. 'It's been in the same place for the last four years that he's been part of our family.' The more we looked at her son's foundation systems, the clearer it became: he knew exactly where the door frame was, but what he didn't know was where his body started and finished, and what better way to find out than by bumping into something.

- *Stamping* – a child with an underdeveloped proprioceptive system might also stamp heavily as they move around and this might be particularly noticeable when they're coming down the stairs. I often hear parents describe this as it sounding like a herd of elephants! Again, if we think about this, if you've not got enough core stability, you're not completely sure where your foot is, and you don't know how much pressure or force this movement requires, then stamping your feet on the stairs seems like a very practical solution!

- *Falling over* – having very little idea of where your body is and not getting reliable messages about how much pressure or force to use in a movement means that we also see children falling over a lot. Parents and carers often describe them as tripping over thin air, because, in terms of the external environment, there's nothing that could cause them to fall.

- *Lack of bilateral integration and sequencing* – not using both sides of the body in an integrated way.

- *Upper body and legs out of sequence with each other* – this can probably be seen most easily when children run. Going back to Usain Bolt (and probably our own running as well), the arms should be a helpful and integrated part of the movement: the right arm working at the same time as the left leg, pumping in time and pushing the body forwards. This is the thing that I find children with underdeveloped systems are most able to explain when I ask them how they think their bodies are working. They often say that they hate running because their arms just go all over the place. One girl said that she felt like an octopus when she ran; her arms seemed as if they had a life of their own and just flapped around. But being able to run around and play chasing and catching games are such an important part of childhood. For developing children, activities like this are a feast for their vestibular system because of the change of pace and direction. For children who have experienced developmental trauma and who are out of synch with themselves on a bodily level, these kind of activities can feel impossible. We need to build core vestibular and proprioceptive functioning to enable them to take part.

Chapter 13

Assessing the Development of the Proprioceptive System

F OR children whose proprioceptive systems are underdeveloped, there are two main functions of the system to consider:

- *Quality of movement* – how smooth, well coordinated and synchronized is the movement? By synchronized, I mean how well the body works as one unit: upper body and legs working together, right and left sides working together. It's important to think about shoulder girdle strength because it gives such good information about the balance of the body, upper body and legs, as well as left and right. As I've already mentioned, all of this needs to be thought about together with what parents and carers have noticed so that it's not just a snapshot of the child's functioning.

- *Body map* – to what extent is the child relying on their eyes to get information about where their body is and what it's doing? Are they getting the messages about body position and how much pressure or force to use in a movement from the muscles and joints?

Activities to notice proprioceptive functioning

The activities that were helpful in assessing the development of the vestibular system are also useful when thinking about the proprioceptive system. We need to revisit the drawing, tightrope walking, going up and down stairs and jumping from cushion to cushion activities, thinking about what information we can glean from them about the proprioceptive system. We should then think about activities that give good information about how strong the shoulders are and how well synchronized a body is – things like commando crawling and crawling. I'm hoping that it's helpful, as you get into the way of noticing the functioning of the different foundation systems, to separate them out like this, even though this separation is artificial because the systems are so interdependent.

I find that once people start to think about the idea of children using their eyes to plan and manage their body and how it moves, it suddenly becomes quite obvious, once they know what they are looking for. And so I'm not going to divide the assessment up in the same way as I did with the tactile and vestibular systems, making a separate part of the assessment for this, but I will highlight the parts of the assessment that are most apparent.

Activity 1: Drawing

As well as getting good information about core stability, watching a child draw is invaluable in understanding how well developed their shoulder girdle is, which in turn helps to make sense of what's happening when they're drawing and writing. Remember the principle of the child developing control from their core and then out to the extremities – what is technically called proximal to distal. I have tried to avoid sweeping generalizations in this book so far, but I would say that it's fairly unusual to meet a child who has experienced early adversity and whose shoulder girdle is as strong as it needs to be for their legs and upper body to be well balanced. Even when children have islands of lovely core stability, they can be really weak in their shoulders. Shoulder strength really only builds through lots of experiences of tummy time and creeping/crawling. If a child hasn't gone through those stages, fine motor activities that happen a long way from the core – like using cutlery or handwriting – are so much more challenging. Again with this activity, it's about the process and how the child approaches the task.

Indicators for a child with an underdeveloped proprioceptive system include:

- Uses a whole arm movement to draw. I often talk at training about the clue being in the title – handwriting – not whole-arm or whole-body writing. We should be able to use our hand to write without any other part of our body moving.

- Either grips the pencil so tightly that they're gouging through the paper, or has such a light grasp of the pencil that they can't use it effectively to make a mark on the paper.

- Clamps their writing arm to the side of their body.

- Copes with changing direction in their writing or drawing by turning the paper rather than being able to control that movement from their pencil.

- Does lots of moving round and changing position – as if they're trying to get lots of additional sensory input so that their body knows where it is.

It's also important to notice what the non-writing hand is doing. Does it look as if it's part of the same body/movement, or does it seem very detached from the rest of the body?

If children are interested in the idea of underdeveloped systems and thinking about how their body works, I often suggest that we pretend we're detectives, trying to find the things about their body that work fantastically well, and the parts that we could help to work even better. If a child is clearly struggling with drawing and writing, I suggest that we put on our detective hats and find out why. We get a very important clue from the next activity, being on the floor, because that helps us to look at how strong their head, neck, shoulder girdle and trunk are. This leads us nicely into moving on to the floor to look at how their body manages lying in a straight line and prone extension.

NADIA, ELSA, SEAN AND AMBER: HOW DRAWING ADDED TO THE PICTURE OF VESTIBULAR AND PROPRIOCEPTIVE FUNCTIONING

NADIA

It's helpful to think about Nadia here, because when she was sitting down to draw, she was really fidgety and squirmy. At that point in the assessment, it was hard to know whether she was wriggling because she didn't have enough core stability to stay sitting upright, or because she had very little sense of where her body was and was moving to keep track of it. It wasn't until we did the lying on our tummies and prone extension, and I could see that she had the beginnings of lovely core stability, that I knew that her wriggling was part of an underdeveloped proprioceptive system rather than a weak core.

ELSA

You might remember that Elsa fell off the chair when she was drawing, and again it would be important to wonder whether this was about core stability or that she wasn't getting the messages about where she was from her muscles and joints. In Elsa's case, when we did the lying on her tummy and prone extension, we could see that her core stability was really weak, and so rebuilding that was going to be an important part of her programme of activities. Until she had better core stability, it was too difficult to work out the proprioceptive aspect of her wobbliness.

SEAN

When Sean was sitting at the table to write, he was leaning completely across the table, moving his whole arm and body as he drew. He was pressing down so hard with the pencil that we could see the imprint of his picture a few pages down the pile. Having to lean across the table and use his whole body to do the drawing were both indicators of poor core stability. Not being able to accurately gauge how much pressure or force to use with his pencil was a sign of an underdeveloped proprioceptive system.

AMBER

It was a very similar picture with Amber. I just needed to gather more information about the proprioceptive system to know where to get started!

Activity 2: Tightrope walking

You'll remember this from the assessment of the vestibular system. I start this with two ropes and gauge whether or not to move on to one rope from how well the child is able to manage two. As well as all of the information about core stability and gravitational security, this is a great exercise for noticing whether children are getting information about body position from their muscles and joints.

When I'm giving the instructions and demonstrating this activity, I don't direct the child's gaze. I show them what to do (and look at the end of the rope as I walk along it), and ask them to copy this. I let them do this a few times, just noticing how they're doing it and where they're looking. I'm interested in a number of things:

- Are they looking down at their feet? It's important to differentiate between a head that's looking down because of a weak vestibular system and a head that's down because a child is needing to watch their feet. A helpful way to do this is to ask them to look up at their parent or carer (who is at the other end of the tightrope, holding it in place) and for them to do something while the child is walking along the rope. If the child loses all core stability and becomes very wobbly, that's a good indication that we need to do more work on core strength and stability (vestibular system). If they lose their footing on the rope or start stamping down very heavily, then I know that working on the proprioceptive system will be helpful.

- Are their feet landing on the rope each time? Does this seem to be more about balance and control or being able to feel the rope?

- Are they stamping heavily? Does this seem to be because they don't really know where their feet are or they can't feel the rope?

SEAN, NADIA, ELSA AND AMBER: THE ROLE OF TIGHTROPE WALKING IN BUILDING A PICTURE OF VESTIBULAR AND PROPRIOCEPTIVE FUNCTIONING

SEAN

The way Sean slid his feet along the rope and looked at his feet while he was rushing along the rope gave important information about his proprioceptive system. You might remember that when I put a few obstacles on the rope for him to step over, he just trod on them. When I asked him to look up at his dad as he was walking along, he kept walking, but his feet weren't on the rope at all and he didn't seem to notice that they weren't. So with Sean we were building up a picture of two systems that were really underdeveloped!

NADIA

Watching Nadia tightrope walk was useful in confirming the picture that was already forming: she had islands of good functioning in some of her foundation systems and gaps in others. Her body was nice and upright while she was walking (some nice postural control and core stability), but she was reluctant to take her feet off the rope (gravitational insecurity) and when I put obstacles down for her to step over, she started putting her feet down much more heavily (proprioceptive – not getting enough messages about position and how much pressure or force to use from the muscles and joints).

ELSA

With Elsa, it was a similar picture to Sean, but with slightly better core stability and sense of where her feet were. So her systems were a bit further along in terms of their development, but still nowhere near where she needed them to be. I was able to slow Elsa down quite easily and could see her get a bit more wobbly when she was walking along, but what was most apparent was that she had very little sense of where her feet were and was only using the ball of her foot rather than her whole foot.

AMBER

I didn't do tightrope walking with Amber because I already had enough information to get started and wasn't wanting to compound her sense of not being able to do things.

Activity 3: Walking down a flight of stairs

You might remember from Chapter 10 that Sean, Nadia, Elsa and Amber were all looking at their feet as they came down the stairs and, just as I described with tightrope walking, it's helpful to try and differentiate the extent to which this is an underdeveloped vestibular system or proprioceptive system.

As we discussed when thinking about the vestibular system, if a child over the age of four is holding on to the banister with two hands and looking at their feet, then I might suggest they try just holding on with one hand coming down the last few steps. If, with a bit of practice, they can manage with just one hand (and by manage I mean they don't lose all core stability, don't trip or get very 'stampy') then I'll suggest they try without holding on at all.

If a child is stamping very heavily as they come down the stairs, I'll suggest that we pretend we're trying to creep down without anyone being able to hear us. Or that there are egg shells on the stairs and we're trying not to break them. I'm curious to see if, with more attention on what they're doing, the child is better able to modulate their stepping.

If a child is watching their feet, then once I've established that they can come down the stairs without being too wobbly or it being too precarious, I might ask them to look at me instead of their feet so that I can get an idea about proprioceptive functioning. With all of these, I want to watch what happens on a bodily level as they try and make the change. Do they lose core stability? Do they need to get more information from their body about where it is? And at the same time, I need to be noticing how a child is feeling about the challenge and whether what I'm asking them to do is too difficult to contemplate, never mind to do.

I find that children are usually pretty clear about whether they're okay to try this or not, and I always follow their lead. They might be quite delighted with themselves that they've managed to come down only holding on with one hand, or they might have found it a bit scary and be quite overwhelmed and uncomfortable. There's really no rush and this is where we come back to the idea of understanding the interplay between the foundation systems and pacing the intervention differently for each child and situation. Some children's foundation systems will have enough islands of good functioning to be able to make it harder straightaway, but others in the same situation might be anxious and fearful and so making it harder might not be the right thing to do.

SEAN, AMBER, ELSA, NADIA AND MICHAELA: DISENTANGLING THE SYSTEMS – TAILORING THE ASSESSMENT FOR EACH INDIVIDUAL CHILD

SEAN

As you may remember, Sean wasn't able to walk down the flight of stairs. He came down the first half on his bottom and then jumped down the last half. He really wasn't keen to go back up and try coming down again, and I think for him he was so used to coming down as fast as he could, even if it was fairly precarious, that it would have felt unfair to expose the weaknesses in his systems. I already knew that there were big gaps in his vestibular system and that we could easily spend the first month concentrating on that before revisiting the stairs.

AMBER

It was a similar picture with Amber; she was clinging so hard to the banister that I didn't want to ask her to try doing it a different way until we'd had the chance to build vestibular functioning.

ELSA

Elsa, however, was quite wobbly (vestibular system) but by this stage in the assessment she was happy to try a few variations on coming down a flight of stairs. We tried coming down only holding on to the banister with one hand and then not holding on at all, before I asked her to look at me as she was coming down those last few steps. As well as highlighting the gaps in her vestibular system, it was also helpful to see that her body quite quickly got the idea that she could get the messages about where her feet were from the muscles and joints rather than her eyes (proprioceptive system). By the time she had come down looking at me rather than her feet five times, she was feeling much more comfortable and confident about doing it, and was keen to go and practise at home. For Elsa, it was going to be possible to work on rebuilding vestibular and proprioceptive systems at the same time.

NADIA

It was much the same with Nadia, and I'm sure that even just having an island of better functioning in terms of core stability gave her the confidence to try the same things as Elsa. When Nadia first came down the stairs, she held on to the banister and watched her feet. When I asked her if she wanted to try coming down without holding on, she was keen to try. It was great to see that, although she became a bit unbalanced initially, her core remained strong, and with lots of repetitions she quite quickly got better at it and we could try her coming down looking at me instead of her feet. Again, I could see that although it took a bit of practice, she was getting a good stable base from her vestibular system and we could focus on proprioceptive functioning.

MICHAELA

I met a 15-year-old girl called Michaela recently and, watching her go up a flight of stairs with her hands on each step in front of her as she went, I got a good idea that we were going to need to do some work on stairs! Sure enough, when she turned round to come down, she held on to the banister really tightly with one hand, the wall with the other hand, and watched her feet every step of the way. When I asked her to try coming down the last couple of steps without holding on, she looked quite anxious, and as soon as she took her hands off the banister she slipped. We'd already done the vestibular part of the assessment and I knew that Michaela had good core stability and gravitational security, and so it was more likely that the difficulties were in the proprioceptive system.

This is one part of the assessment where I often notice a big difference in what you can do with older children. It was useful to be able to explain to Michaela and her foster carer that she wasn't getting the messages from her muscles and joints but that it didn't mean there was anything broken about her body, it was just that she hadn't been in a place as a small child where her brain could develop those pathways. The idea that the pathways weren't broken but just hadn't been discovered gave her the confidence to start that process of rebuilding her proprioceptive system. We talked about challenging her body by not letting her use her eyes to find her feet and legs, and she was keen to try it. We then spent the next half an hour on the stairs, just gradually working our way from her holding on to the banister with two hands and watching her feet, to using one then no banisters, and then looking at her foster carer as she walked down. This was a slow, tentative process to start with, but Michaela was keen to keep trying and so we just kept going, until she wasn't having to concentrate so hard on every movement and it was beginning to feel okay to her. We even got to the point of her feeling confident to try coming down the last two steps with her eyes closed, which was so far from where we started that we were all quite delighted with what we'd managed to achieve! Stopping at that point was good and Michaela and her foster carer were keen to keep practising that as often as they could.

Activity 4: Jumping from cushion to cushion

In considering what this activity can help us notice about proprioceptive functioning, we can see the extent to which the body works as an integrated unit. There are two main things to look out for here:

- Which part of the body is leading the movement? This may sound a bit of a strange idea to start with, but if you try jumping along a line and watch yourself in a mirror, you should see that it's your head that leads the movement.

Not that your head is miles in front of your body, but it is still leading. What I often notice in children with underdeveloped proprioceptive systems is that their feet lead and their head follows. This is probably most noticeable when you introduce a change of direction and they're zig zagging across the cushions. If you've ever watched the Wallace and Gromit film, *The Wrong Trousers*, you'll know very clearly what I mean by the legs leading the movement. (It's a great film, definitely one of our family favourites!)

• What are the arms doing? We want arms to be an integral part of the movement, moving in a helpful way, being part of the power and stability as the child jumps forwards. Is this how it looks, or are the arms trailing behind? Or are they flapping or moving around in a way that isn't a helpful part of the movement? Think all the time about whether the body is working as one synchronized unit – are there any anomalies? Remember the girl in Chapter 11 who described herself as feeling like an octopus when she ran, not able to control her arms at all, never mind them being a helpful part of the movement.

Activities to notice whether the body is working as one unit

Let's move on now to the activities that provide information about the extent to which the body is working as a synchronized unit: upper body and legs, and right and left sides working together. Commando crawling and crawling are perfect for doing this – and again I'd urge you to try doing these yourself and to watch typically developing children doing this.

Activity 1: Commando crawling

In the sequential progression of development, commando crawling comes after the baby is able to prop themselves up on one arm and reach for a toy, and before they reach the dizzy heights of crawling. It's usually that stage before they're able to hold themselves in a crawling position and when it's still their shoulders and arms that have the most power. If you watch babies at this stage, you'll see that every so often their legs try to get involved, but generally it knocks them off balance and they overshoot the movement. The upper body reigns supreme at this stage.

When I'm doing an assessment, I always do commando crawling after we've been lying on our tummies. I make sure that children understand we're going to crawl forwards on our tummies using only our arms to move us along. I say that this is really hard, but let's just try and see how we do. At this stage, when I want to notice how they do it, I don't say much more than this, but just see if we can commando crawl along together.

You may be familiar with the experience of trying out a new activity with a friend and being a bit gutted that they are a lot better at it than you are (definitely my experience with pilates!) and it's useful to remember that feeling here. I never go ahead of a child, and I tell parents that we'll just go at the child's pace so that they don't get a sense of failing or not even being able to do it as well as their aged therapist!

I am observing the child as they are doing this:

- What is their head position like? I know this is going back to the vestibular system and core stability, but it's another great chance to see whether they are holding their head up and looking where they are going.

- Where is the power for the movement coming from? Are they able to pull themselves forwards with their arms? For some children, no matter how hard they try, they can't do this and so I just stop there. For others, they are determined to get themselves moving and so do everything they can to make this happen. Sometimes children put their arms down by their sides and try to push themselves forwards; other times they use their legs to power the movement. At this stage, I want to build up a picture of how they do it, so I just notice this.

It's very rare to meet a child whose systems are underdeveloped but who can commando crawl at the pace and for as long as you'd see a typically developing child managing to. But again, there's no need for a child to know how they compare to their peers – all I want to know is what their best attempt today is, because that gives me a starting point. It's also important to remember that parents often won't have an idea of what to expect in terms of commando crawling (it's interesting to hear Nadia's mum talk about this in Chapter 17). This is especially true for adoptive parents who adopted their child when they were already walking. But again, my job is to help them notice the disparity between legs and upper body strength, and feel confident with the idea of trying to close that gap. I usually talk to children about how practising this and getting even stronger and faster at it will really help with other things, like managing cutlery and handwriting.

ALISHA: A CHILD'S DESCRIPTION OF AN UNDERDEVELOPED PROPRIOCEPTIVE SYSTEM

I met Alisha, who was eight years old, when she and her foster carer came to see me for an assessment. I asked her if she knew why she was coming to see me. She didn't seem to know, so I said that I was someone who worked with children and was interested in helping them to get their bodies working as well as they possibly could. I asked her how she thought her body worked, whether it did what she needed it to do, or if there was anything she found difficult. Alisha looked at me very seriously and said, 'Yes, Sarah, I think I've got a blockage.' Not at all sure what might be coming next, I asked if she could explain it a bit more. She said that she thought she had some sort of blockage between her brain and her hand, because in her head she could see what she wanted her hand to do when it was writing, but it didn't come out the way she could see in her head. I thought that was a brilliant explanation and suggested we be detectives and see if we could solve the mystery. She thought that sounded a good idea, and we made a start on the assessment.

I could see that Alisha had some islands of lovely vestibular functioning, but when we came to commando crawling, she wasn't able to make herself move forwards at all. I talked to her about how she needed to have strong shoulders to be able to write, and that it wasn't so much a blockage as a bit of her body that wasn't as strong as she needed it to be, but that she and her mum could easily sort it out by doing some activities five or six times every day.

I gave Alisha and her foster carer four different activities to build her shoulder girdle, including commando crawling. I was so delighted for her when I saw her again a month later and she was proudly holding her 'pen licence' that meant she could use a pen instead of a pencil at school.

Activity 2: Crawling

Crawling is a lovely familiar activity, but, as you're probably getting to realize by now, it's actually a complex task. I'm often surprised how hard it is to notice everything I need to when a child is crawling. If a parent or carer has brought in a recording of their child crawling, I usually have to watch it a number of times before I can make sense of what's happening.

- *Starting from the top* – head position. If a child is looking down towards the floor or at their hands, I want to understand why. It could be an underdeveloped vestibular system (not enough strength in their neck and shoulders to keep their head looking forwards) or it may be that they need to be able to see their hands to know where they are and what they're doing (proprioceptive system).

- *Arms* – is the child able to have their arms straight as they crawl, so that weight is going from the shoulder down to the wrist? Sometimes, if a child has a very underdeveloped vestibular system, their limbs can be very floppy and it can be too hard in the early stages for them to get into this position. If that's the case, then building core stability will be the best starting point.

- *Hands* – we want flat hands, fingers facing forwards. So if a child is doing anything else with their hands, I just correct the position. I've seen all sorts of different ways of doing it (fists clenched, making a bridge with their hands), but we need to get those hands flat on the floor so that their weight is going through their wrist and they're strengthening the arches of their hands, as well as the finger extensors. If a child is making a fist with their hand as they're crawling along, it may be that there are still vestiges of that palmar reflex present. In that case, I'd also suggest activities for the family to do to help with that.

- *Right and left sides of the body together* – we want to see children crawling where the right hand and left leg move together, and the left hand and right leg move together (bilateral integration and sequencing). When children aren't able to do this, they often move both hands together, then do a kind of a skip to bring their legs forward. This is often done at top speed. If a child is doing this, I might suggest that we go back to tummy time and commando crawling for a few weeks and make sure that we get to the stage of them using alternating arms before I come back to crawling. At other times, I might suggest we do bear walking, where we put our hands and feet on the ground, legs as straight as we can, and try to walk along like that. Again, because of its unfamiliarity, it's a good way for me to see whether the right and left sides are working together.

- *Speed* – crawling at top speed covers a whole array of difficulties and if a child is going so fast that I can't see what's happening, then I need to try and slow things down. Sometimes I ask the child to try crawling backwards and, because it's unfamiliar, they tend to go more slowly, which gives me more time to try and work out what's happening. At other times we might pretend to be explorers out in the jungle, perhaps doing a night time check of the camp, so needing to creep along really slowly and carefully so as not to disturb anything.

SEAN, ELSA, AMBER AND NADIA: THE CHALLENGES OF CRAWLING

SEAN

Sean struggled with crawling. He had his hands in a fist and crawled by putting both hands forwards and then jumping his legs in.

ELSA

Elsa struggled, too. As well as having her hands in a fist, she wasn't able to get her arms straight because her muscle tone was too low.

AMBER

I didn't ask Amber to try crawling as I'd got enough information before we came to that part of the assessment.

NADIA

Nadia was almost able to manage crawling; her head was in a good position, her hands were flat with fingers facing forwards, and her arms were lovely and straight. The only bit she struggled with was the bilateral integration and sequencing. To help get her started with this, I put a big, thick sock on her right foot and took her sock off her left foot. We also put a mitten on her left hand, and she then tried crawling, moving the hand and foot with the mitten and sock on at the same time. This extra sensory input really helped her to begin to get the right movement, and once she'd got it, after a bit of practising, she was able to keep doing it without the socks.

Chapter 14

Rebuilding Underdeveloped Vestibular and Proprioceptive Systems

I N this chapter, I will talk through some of the games and activities the BUSS model uses to develop vestibular and proprioceptive functioning. Children who have experienced developmental trauma will usually have a patched together kind of system, and I'm always keen to make sure this doesn't continue. I'm aiming to support families to build really solid foundations, even if that takes a while. It can be tempting to want to move on quickly and to do things that seem more complex, but a slow and steady start is absolutely the best way of doing it. Think back to those babies – no one would think of enrolling a pre-walking child in ice-skating classes. They need to have the basics in place before they can do more complicated things.

This means making sure that a child is really proficient at each stage and that it's not a fleeting thing the child can occasionally manage to do if they're in a particular frame of mind. Every child is different, but where there are gaps in the system, I much prefer to take children back to the start of that system and rebuild from there, so I'm confident that we've got a good solid base. I tend to err on the side of assuming that it's unlikely any child who has experienced early adversity will have good enough foundation systems. Even if there are islands of good functioning, I want to make sure that everything is working as well as it possibly can – so we're aiming high and not being content with good enough or better than it used to be.

In observing how typically developing babies spend so much of their waking hours moving within loving relationships, we can see how impossible it is for babies who have been neglected to have had nearly as much connection and stimulation as they need to get their brains and bodies developing as well as they could. Suzanne Zeedyk is a brilliant psychologist working in Scotland, and her website,[1] 'The Connected Baby',[2] offers a wealth of interesting and helpful information around the relational side of this stage of development – and I hope by now you understand the importance of all of the movement that happens alongside that.

Getting started

With a few rare exceptions, I usually start rebuilding under-developed vestibular and proprioceptive systems with what I think of as the magic three – tummy time, commando crawling and regular crawling. This might not seem a lot, but along with two or three activities from the tactile system, it quickly adds up and it is important not to overwhelm families. Sometimes, children are raring to go and a family can easily do more activities. At other times, it's a matter of reining things back and not giving any more activities even if there seems to be endless capacity. Getting these right is the best foundation to enable a child to move forward. So, as with grading individual activities, it is important to find out what's right for each family.

Tummy time

There is no better starting point than tummy time. It sounds too simple and people often get into a muddle because they want it to be more complicated, but trust me when I say that we can start to shift things just by getting children and young people lying in a good position on their tummies. Because we're rebuilding an underdeveloped system and not treating a sensory processing disorder, we need to follow, as closely as we can, the blueprint of typical development. And this

1   www.suzannezeedyk.com
2   http://connectedbaby.net

has to involve lots of floor time. So while the activity itself may be simple, the challenge for parents and carers can often be how to make it fun and interesting. We need the child to spend a lot of time doing this – it's not a once a week kind of thing. I'm sure that all the parents and carers I've worked with would support me in saying that the best way to help children to spend time on their tummies is to make it fun. So whatever it is that a child is going to play or do on their on their tummy, it has to be something that's appealing to that child. Having the child engaged in the activity allows you a bit of space to notice and focus on technique.

If we think about children like Elsa and Nadia, who were able to get into a straight line when they were lying on their tummies, it's a nice easy starting point to have them lying on their tummies for as much time as is possible. There are so many things that children can do lying on their tummies: watch TV, read, play board games, play on a tablet or Xbox, chat, play cars – all sorts of things. Even though this sounds such a simple and familiar activity, there are a few things to pay attention to:

- *Head position* – we want heads looking forwards or up, never down. So if a child is playing with an iPad while they're lying on their tummy, I make sure it is propped up on a cushion so that the child's eye line is up rather than looking at the floor. If you watch a baby on their tummy, they might well be looking at a toy in front of them, but their head will never be hanging down the way you see in children whose foundation systems are underdeveloped.

- *Shoulders and arms* – ideally, I want children to be lying on their tummies and supporting themselves on their bent arms, so that their chest is just lifted off the floor. But if this is uncomfortable for a child (and, unless there's a medical reason, this is usually just because it is unfamiliar), then it's fine for them to have a cushion under their chest to support themselves. Remember the idea of constantly grading activities. If the first task is to get the child feeling comfortable on their tummy, then I do that, and when the child is feeling okay being on their tummy, I can think with the family more about technique. If I use props like a cushion under their chest until they get comfortable being in that position, it's important to keep reviewing whether it's still needed and take it away as soon as it isn't. Again, just thinking about the idea of grading, it might be too big a leap for a child to go from having a cushion under their chest to just being on the floor, but swapping being propped up on the cushion to lying on a soft, cosy rug will mean that their body is having to do more work, but they'll still feel a bit supported.

- *Hips* – before we move to lying down, I usually make sure children know where their hip bones are. Then when they're on their tummies, I ask them to feel and see if both hip bones are touching the floor. This helps me (and the child) to know that they're lying in a nicely aligned position, and not veering off to either side.

- *Legs* – these are a bit less important here, but I try to make sure that the child's leg position isn't throwing them off balance. I aim for a straight line from the crown of the child's head to between their feet. But it really doesn't matter if the child's legs are straight or they've got their lower leg bent up, as long as overall they're in a straight line.

If we think about children like Sean and Amber, who were struggling to get into a straight line on their tummies, then the first step is to provide a bit of scaffolding.

With younger children, like Sean, I find it works best to use parents or carers to get the child into the right position, so that all three are lying on their tummies, with the child in the middle. This worked well for Sean. It's helpful for parents and carers to think of themselves as the scaffolding, because they need to be close enough in to the child to be holding the child's body in a lovely straight line. It's a bit like watching parents hold a tiny baby, when the baby is lying on the parent's chest and they've got their hand on the baby's back – because the baby is so tiny at that stage, their hand almost covers the whole baby, building that

baby's sense of where they are (and well-being) in relation to the parent. When I'm describing this position of lying on their tummy between their parents to children, I often talk to about them being the hot dog in a roll. If, like Sean, a child is really squirmy when they're lying like this, I suggest putting a nice heavy blanket over all three people, just to try and settle things down. In proprioceptive terms, we think of the child squirming because they're trying to get more feedback from the environment about where their body is, so by putting a heavy blanket on top of them, we're maximizing the amount of sensory input. If their body can feel where it is, it doesn't have to keep moving around as much. In this position, the child should know where each part of their body is – their tummy, arms and legs are in contact with the ground and the blanket is doing what the parents hand was doing for the tiny baby, giving lots of information about where they are and a reassuring sense that everything is going to be okay.

In single parent or carer families, it's just a matter of adapting things a bit, and using cushions or the side of a sofa to be the other half of the hot dog roll. You can still get that nice cosy, squashed-in feeling that gives plenty of sensory feedback to the child's body.

With older children (or children who don't like the feeling of having someone so close to them), as well as using tactile system games to work on that, I suggest they tuck their feet under the sofa. This gives their body more information about where their legs are and helps them to use that as an anchor to make a straight line from. This was how Amber started; she would watch TV lying on her tummy with her legs tucked under the sofa. But it is crucial to keep remembering the importance of the relational context of development; the baby brain needs an attuned adult brain to develop alongside, so even if a young person is able to do this themselves, I still want parents or carers to be around. This is partly to make sure the child's body is in a straight line and not swerving off to one side or the other, but it's also a lot about giving encouragement and emotional support. Being in this position will feel very different and often quite strange for young people and I never underestimate the importance of having someone encouraging and helping with that feeling.

THE ROLE TUMMY TIME CAN PLAY
IN BUILDING CORE STABILITY

Because asking a child to lie on their tummy seems so simple, it's easy to underestimate its impact. I met Emma and Andy, who are adoptive parents. They had recently attended BUSS training and had been doing some tactile system games as well as tummy time. It was interesting to hear Emma describe the changes she had noticed in relation to her daughter sitting on a chair:

> Before she would sit half on, half off the chair, constantly off-balance: her legs would be swinging and she'd always be moving, fidgeting, moving from her bottom onto her knees and back again. We thought this was an attention issue, or hypervigilance. Then we came on the training and we thought that maybe it wasn't!
>
> We've been doing tummy time every day, as often as we can – so when she and her brother watch TV during bedtime routine, they lie on their tummies. In a few weeks, she built from five minutes to half an hour. And what we've noticed is now, when she sits on her chair, her whole bottom is on the chair – she's barely swinging her legs, she's not moving around. What we thought was hypervigilance was in fact a lack of core stability.

The other thing Emma went on to talk about was how much her daughter, who is eight, warmed to the idea of having an underdeveloped system, rather than there being something wrong with her. And with that lovely core stability developing, we could move on to the next stage of things, which for her was building shoulder girdle strength and encouraging her body to work as an integrated unit. Never underestimate the power of tummy time!

Commando crawling

In this collection of three activities to start rebuilding under-developed vestibular and proprioceptive systems, commando crawling is probably the most physically challenging. This is because children have generally got used to being able to move around pretty quickly, on strong legs. With commando crawling,

I'm asking them to use their shoulder girdle to power the movement and that's generally fairly weak in comparison with their legs. So while the activity itself is simple, I find that there needs to be lots of support, encouragement and praise of whatever the child is able to manage, knowing that they will get stronger with practice. It's important that they don't get discouraged – if a child can do one step today, I encourage families to celebrate that with them, and practise that one step as many times as they can, and then the next day it is hoped that they will manage two steps.

It's important to focus on position here. When I was describing the assessment, I said that I was interested to see how the child did commando crawling – but it's different here. They need to be in the correct position to build shoulder girdle strength. So while I might have got good information about how underdeveloped their shoulder was from watching them use their legs to power the movement, now we really need to focus on technique so that this activity improves that.

It's also really important to make sure that a child doesn't hurt themselves while they're commando crawling – no carpet burns or sore arms. Wearing long sleeves (and thicker material like a sweatshirt or even an outdoor coat to start with) can be nicely protective. Some families have used skateboard pads but these tend to be a bit too helpful and provide quite a bit of grip, so if it's possible to use clothes, or even something like a tubigrip, then that's better.

There are lots of ways children's bodies try to help them out with commando crawling, and these are things that it's important to correct:

- Keeping their arms very close to their body, not having them out in front of them, but at their sides.

- Trying to push themselves forwards, rather than pulling themselves forwards. I always think this looks a bit like a fish, with their arms as fins down at the side of their body. Again, this isn't going to help build shoulder strength, so I need to make sure parents understand that they're aiming to have the child's arms out in front of them as they start to crawl. A couple of steps in a good position repeated multiple times a day is better than a child being able to crawl for longer but in a position that isn't building shoulder girdle strength or encouraging their head to be in a nice functional position looking ahead.

- Using both arms together is really just an early stage of commando crawling. If a child is doing this, I encourage them to try alternating arms (more like a front crawl swimming action), at least for part of the time they're commando crawling. I might suggest we try four 'steps' with arms together, then three with alternating arms, then back to arms together, just gradually shifting the balance as the child gets stronger, until eventually they are using alternating arms.

- 'Planting' their elbows into the carpet and pulling themselves along.

- Lifting the tummy up off the floor and then using a swaying hip action to move forwards is sometimes seen if a child has got some core stability. I call it 'snaky hips', but again, I want to encourage the child to have their hips on the floor so that their shoulders are doing all the work. If a child is commando crawling on a laminate or other hard floor (which tends to be easier so is a good place to start), I put a small bean bag under their tummies and the challenge is to try and keep the bean bag under there while they crawl along. If a child is crawling on a carpet, I often put something on their lower back, like a cushion (perhaps pretending to be a tortoise) and the challenge is to keep the cushion on their back while they're crawling.

PETER: DOUBLE TROUSERS!

Given how challenging commando crawling is, and how slowly children are able to do it compared with other activities, I'm always trying to come up with ways to keep it fun and interesting. The best solution to this came (as the best ideas usually do!) from some parents. Their child, Peter, was used to being able to do everything at top speed and found it frustrating to be so slow when he was commando crawling. So they turned it into a different kind of a game – crawl out of your waterproof (and so quite slippy) trousers! Peter would put his waterproof trousers on over whatever he was wearing, and crawl along, keeping his tummy on the floor, until he'd managed to crawl right out of the waterproofs! This made it so much more fun; just changing the emphasis around the purpose of the game helped him to forget that he wasn't going as fast as he usually did.

- Using legs or feet is usually fairly easy to spot, though sometimes it is a bit more subtle than at other times. For some children, balancing something on their (straight) legs can work well. This could be a cushion, a soft toy – whatever works for them. I remember one little boy I met who didn't want to do any of this, and the only things he really liked were his cars and trucks. So we tied some string to one of his trucks to make a tow rope and he was then very happy to crawl along towing his truck, keeping his legs nice and straight so that the truck didn't topple over.

There is a little girl who comes to BUSS gym club who wears a headband for the beam and bars work, and then puts this round her ankles for commando crawling to keep her legs in place. Variations on this are mermaid costumes, a big Christmas sock to fit both feet in, and just holding a child's ankles as they're going along – I usually say I'm giving them a turbo boost!

A good commando crawling position looks like the image on the right – with the child's body in a straight line from the crown of the head to between the heels.

When children are starting to commando crawl, it's important to get a balance of being quite hot on technique and not being so fussy they feel they can't ever get it right. When a child is struggling to move at all, as Sean was, it is important to make it fun and just support them while they try to get moving to start with. If Sean's parents had been focusing too much on technique at that stage, he'd have got really discouraged and given up. Once he was able to take a few 'steps', his parents held his feet and gave him a bit of help to get started. With Nadia, who was able to take a few 'steps' straightaway, I was able to think with her parents about technique right from the start.

I grade commando crawling in four stages – engagement, technique, stamina and speed.

SEAN, ELSA, AMBER, AND NADIA: COMMANDO CRAWLING

SEAN

Sean had struggled to get into a straight line on his tummy and hadn't been able to lift off the ground at all in prone extension. When we came to commando crawling, Sean needed help to get his body into the straight line, and his instinct to start himself moving was to use his legs. His dad did a great job of holding his legs and we could see just how weak his shoulders were; to begin with he couldn't move forwards at all. But Sean was nothing if not determined and so, with his dad holding his ankles and giving a bit of a turbo boost, Sean kept on trying until he managed to take a couple of 'steps' on his own. It was great to see how determined he was and how supportive his parents were. I knew that with this combination it wouldn't be long before he was going to go much further! The challenge was definitely to keep his legs still and let his shoulders do the work.

ELSA

Elsa had been able to get into a straight line on her tummy and get a tiny bit of elevation with prone extension. She was able to get herself into the right position for commando crawling but she couldn't make any progress with it. With lots of help and encouragement from her parents she was able to take a couple of steps but these took a lot of effort and she was tired and discouraged after a very short time.

AMBER

Amber presented a similar picture to Sean, in that she'd struggled to get into a straight line on her tummy and hadn't been able to lift up into prone extension. We started commando crawling from the position on her tummy with her feet tucked under the sofa (which was how she continued to make sure she was in a straight line when she was on her tummy). Initially she wasn't able to move forwards at all, but again, with a good understanding of what she was trying to do and a lot of determination, she gradually managed to move forwards by using both her arms together to pull herself along. We talked about what a huge effort that had been and how it would get easier, but only with a lot of practice. Amber was so keen to get her body working for her that she practised this over and over again over the next couple of weeks, with her mum helping with technique. Noticing head position was important and her mum hid interesting things on the shelves of the bookcase to encourage Amber to look up.

NADIA

Nadia had some islands of good functioning in the core stability part of her vestibular system, so had been able to lie in a straight line and get a bit of elevation with prone extension. This really helped with commando crawling, because her head was in a good functional position, looking where she was going. But she was frustrated that she couldn't go faster, and her mum needed to work hard to hold on to her legs to stop them doing the work. Again, turning this into a different sort of game worked well; we put a heavy cushion on her legs and Nadia pretended to be the tortoise in the tortoise and the hare story, making slow and steady progress as she went.

Regular crawling

As I hope you will remember from Chapter 3, crawling is phenomenally important and this is a great opportunity to revisit that stage and reap the benefits in terms of motor and sensory advances that may not have been acquired at the usual time. However, as you'll see as we go through this section, it's hard to crawl without some good vestibular and proprioceptive functioning. So while crawling may seem easier because it's so familiar, it may be that a child isn't ready to move on to this until they've built a solid foundation of time on their tummy and doing commando crawling. If we think about Sean, Elsa, Nadia and Amber, of these four children it was only Nadia whom I suggested should do crawling in that first month. Sean, Elsa and Amber all had enough work to do getting into a good position on their tummies and developing their head, neck and shoulder strength. I was also keen to get them to the stage of being able to confidently use alternating arms for commando crawling before I introduced crawling.

TRY IT FOR YOUR SELF!

As with all of these activities, it really helps if you can have a go at doing it and really feel, from the inside, what it's like. If possible, have a go at crawling now. I'm assuming that you'll be crawling 'correctly' – alternating hands and with the opposite leg and arm moving together. If this isn't how you crawl, then just try it and see how it feels. It is probably very strange at first – but given that this is a more unusual way of crawling, and doesn't give the benefits of regular crawling, it would be a good idea to watch some typically developing children, because, at the risk of sounding a bit rude, then you'll see how it should be done!

You should notice that you're able to keep your body still while you move your arms and legs. You might even be able to extend your right arm and left leg right out at the same time and hold that position – a lovely co-contraction, a stable core and moving limbs! Now go back to crawling and notice the way your head is positioned so that you can see where you're going. If you watch a baby crawling, their head is almost always looking where they're going and around at things in their path. Now look down at your hands – they should be flat on the ground and your fingers should be out straight and facing forwards. Again, it's worth spending time observing typically developing children so that you get a clear picture in your mind of the stages of crawling. You rarely see babies crawling with their hands clenched, except perhaps in the very early stages, but you do see it a lot when children's foundation systems are underdeveloped, and it's important to be noticing all of these little things that are important to correct.

Next, try and notice how the right and left sides of your body are working together to keep a stable position while you're making good progress forwards. Sometimes when you really focus in on a skill that you can normally do without thinking about it, it all goes to pieces, and if that's what's happening, just start crawling backwards and things should right themselves.

It's important to have this clearly in your head before you watch your child crawl, because you need to notice exactly how they are doing it.

As we discussed in Chapter 12, there are a number of ways children will try to compensate for gaps in their foundation systems. For some of these, like a lack of bilateral integration and sequencing or very low muscle tone in the arms, things are more complicated. But if a child has some core stability and is able have both sides of their body working in a coordinated and integrated way, and is able to crawl with straight arms, then it's a good activity to use. It's important to correct head and hand position, because otherwise you're not going to be building different movement pathways in the brain.

- *Head* – I always encourage children to look where they're going, and to do this they need something interesting to look at as they crawl. I worked with a fantastic teaching assistant once who made a treasure hunt with laminated cards that she stuck around the wall at just the right height. The child had great fun crawling around and gathering clues. With older children, hiding things around the room at the height that means their head is in a good position also works well. I always try to be mindful of keeping it fun and interesting and getting the level of challenge right.

- *Hands* – if a child is making fists with their hands as they crawl or balancing on their thumbs and fingers, then as well as encouraging them to straighten their fingers out so their hands are flat on the floor while they're crawling, I also suggest doing other activities that encourage their hands to be flat and stretched out. Games with Play-Doh® where the child is rolling out the Play-Doh® with a rolling pin (without handles) so that their hands are going over the rolling pin, are great. Or rolling out chapattis, or kneading and stretching out bread dough – all of these are really good. Doing hand prints and making patterns with flat hands and outstretched fingers are also great.

The exceptions...

It's interesting to think about the children who have experienced developmental trauma and who, at first glance, look as if they've got good balance and coordination. Generally, they are the children whose parents and carers say that they're doing really well in sport and they're not sure if they need this kind of intervention. And on one level they may be right, but I always think it's worth going through the assessment to make sure that all of the systems are as well developed as they need to be, and that they're in balance with each other. Typically, there are some islands of really good vestibular functioning, and this might be good core stability and balance. So they might skip up the stairs and move around in a way that looks very smooth and well coordinated. Generally, it's only when I ask them to do commando crawling, tightrope walking or to walk down the stairs that the gaps begin to show. I worked with a lovely family recently who were astonished when we got to the commando crawling part of the assessment. They couldn't believe how hard their son found commando crawling – he was in a cricket team and doing all sorts of sporty things, but had very little strength in his shoulders.

Going down a flight of stairs also elicits useful information about the extent to which these children may be using their eyes to track their movements. There is not the hugely unstable feel about this that there is with children whose vestibular systems are also underdeveloped, which makes it much easier to work on, as I've already talked about with Michaela in Chapter 13. For these children, watching their feet is indicative of the process of development having been from their feet up rather than from their heads down; that muddle of development means that while there are islands of better functioning, their body has missed the stages of pre-crawling and crawling. Both of these stages are so important in the child 'practising' movement before it happens – you can watch a baby rocking backwards and forwards on their hands and knees, testing out how much pressure or force to use, often overshooting the movement, before they move forwards in a crawl. These are such important stages in building the internal body map, and so for these 'exception' children, who have good vestibular functioning but little sense of where their body is or how much pressure or force to use in a movement (proprioceptive functioning), I suggest they do lots of other things without looking at what they're doing to try and build that map.

MICHAELA: BUILDING AN INTERNAL BODY MAP

Let's think a bit more about Michaela. After we'd finished going up and down the stairs, we all sat down together to have a well-deserved snack. I asked Gary, her foster carer, to put Michaela's drink and snack (some biscuits) in the usual place at the table, and for Michaela to sit down as usual. But then I asked her to close her eyes and to see if she could eat her biscuits and drink her milk with her eyes closed. I think that the snack probably took a bit longer than usual, but it was fun and another way of encouraging Michaela's brain to get the messages about body position and how much pressure or force to use in a movement from her muscles and joints rather than her eyes. She really enjoyed doing this, so when she'd finished we went outside and played some more games like that. She tried walking with her eyes closed for five steps to see if she could stay in a straight line, then increased it as she realized she could. We tried Gary standing a distance from her, and Michaela closing her eyes and walking towards him, stopping just before she thought she was going to bump into him – all to try and help her body build that map of itself from the inside. But remember, we could only move on so quickly because Michaela had good core stability – without that, we'd have been starting on the floor.

The great thing about children who have islands of good functioning in one system is that it is generally quicker and easier to grow the less well-developed system. So Michaela and the boy who I mentioned who was a good cricketer both had good core stability and gravitational security (vestibular system) and both were able to very quickly build speed and stamina in doing things with their eyes closed and crawling/commando crawling (proprioceptive system). I find that usually I only need to see children like this for an assessment and one follow-up session – by that time they're usually much more balanced in terms of their vestibular and proprioceptive systems, and able to continue to build capacity through the usual opportunities available to children. I encourage involvement in activities like gymnastics, which are a great way to continue to nurture the development of these systems, as well as being good fun.

Even rarer exceptions

Very occasionally I might meet a child who, in spite of appalling early adversity, is in great physical shape. I remember doing an assessment of a seven-year-old girl and stopping the assessment after she'd flown through the floor-based work, at the point where she was demonstrating her (beautifully controlled) front and back flips followed by her handstands and cartwheels. But she's the only child I've seen like that in the last six years. I think her mum was a bit puzzled by how excited I was as I told them that they definitely didn't need to see me and gave them some information about gymnastics and dance classes that I thought she might enjoy. The little girl was delighted!

Chapter 15

And Breathe: A Chance to Catch Up

F ROM the conversations I've had with people as I've been writing this book, the overwhelming demand has been for lots of examples of children and young people. I've tried to use as many examples as I can, but I appreciate that it's a lot of children to keep track of and might feel a bit confusing at times! The purpose of this chapter is to look at the information that the assessment has given about two of those children, Sean and Elsa. As well as just getting all of the information in one place for you, I want to think a bit more about their presentation and why, even though they looked fairly similar, the emphasis in their programmes at the beginning was quite different. I'll take you through the assessment session, the activities for the first month and what the parents reported when I met with them a month later. Then in Chapter 16 we'll follow their progress through the second stage of the programme. Both families (and their children's schools) were part of the four-stage BUSS intervention and had come on the 'Introduction to the BUSS Model' training day at the beginning of our work together.

Chapter 17 gives the chance to hear from Amber and Nadia's parents about the programmes they started with and how they developed.

I want to emphasize that although the BUSS model can seem quite simple, there are always a lot of things going on, which is why there is accredited training and supervision to support practitioners as they develop their skills. Although physical activities are the vehicle the BUSS model uses to build underdeveloped systems, there needs to be careful thought and consideration to make sure that the child's sense of themselves on an emotional level, the relationship between the child and parent or carer, and the parent or carer's capacity (emotionally and practically) are all in the mix when planning an intervention. Just throwing a raft of activities that should work to build an underdeveloped system doesn't work nearly as effectively as tailoring a programme to an individual child and family. And if you don't get the level of challenge right, you risk compounding the child's (and family's) sense of failure and it can make it much more difficult to keep going.

Sean's assessment

Let's start with the main points. As you might remember, Sean was six years old when I met him.

Tactile system

- *Feely bag* – Sean wanted to use his eyes, quite 'crashy' and 'bangy' in his movements, rushing around.

- *Touch games* – Sean was over responding to touch and got very wriggly and squirmy when mum was drawing shapes on his back.

- *Taste games* – he could tell the same/different but not two flavours together.

Vestibular system

- *Lying on tummy* – Sean found it really hard to get his body in a straight line on the ground.

- *Prone extension* – Sean wasn't able to lift his upper body, but with dad holding his feet he managed a tiny bit of elevation.

- *Stairs* – he was really tentative, holding on, looking down, wanting to jump.

- *Leaping* – he couldn't land on the cushions, lots of falling over, landing on his knees.

Proprioceptive system

- *Sitting drawing* – Sean's forearms were completely on the table and he tilted his body as he moved his whole arm to do the movement. He pressed really hard; the imprint was visible a few pages down.

- *Commando crawling* – he used his legs, but was fantastically determined and with his parents holding/pushing his legs, he was able to try a couple of 'steps'.

- *Tightrope walking* – he looked at his feet, sliding along the rope.

- *Picture of a whole person* – I thought that this picture below spoke volumes about Sean's sense of himself on a bodily level, and found myself imagining how it might feel to try and move around with a body that looked so cumbersome and awkward.

I also noted a lovely warm relationship and how positive and encouraging his parents were. They were very good at keeping pace with Sean and gently trying to bring him back to what we wanted him to be doing.

Starting programme for the first four weeks
Tactile system
Trying to build discriminatory functioning and slow things down to help Sean to stay in the moment of an experience for a bit longer.

- Touch games.

- 'Mouthly' games, including taste games, blowing bubbles and straw games.
- Feely bag games.

Vestibular system
Aiming to build core strength and stability.

- Tummy time.
- Prone extension.

Proprioceptive system
Aiming to build shoulder girdle strength to lessen the huge disparity between his legs and his upper body. I was also hoping to encourage his body to be less reliant on his eyes for information about where his body was and what it was doing – I wanted it to get those messages from the muscles and joints.

- Commando crawling.
- Tightrope walking, starting with two ropes.

Review session with parents four weeks after the assessment
The first thing that Sean's parents said to me was, 'Sean is loving the challenges, especially the milk challenge and the commando crawling challenge.' They had brought videos of him doing the activities, which was very helpful as I could really focus on technique and get an idea of speed and stamina as I reviewed the different systems.

Tactile system
The family were drinking everything with straws! Sean's strength and stamina had really increased and he could now drink yogurts and thick milkshakes through straws.

Vestibular system

- *Tummy time* – they had done lots of this and Sean was now choosing to lie on his tummy for lots of things.

- *Prone extension* – his parents said that Sean could now get good elevation and hold it steadily. He practised this at least four times a day!

Proprioceptive system

- *Commando crawling* – Sean's parents could see that this was getting stronger and faster. He could now get about half way across a room before he started to use his legs. I noticed from the recordings they brought that his head still tended to be down. We talked about giving him something to do that would mean he was looking up rather than at the floor, and his parents thought that he'd enjoy a treasure hunt where the clues were just above skirting board height.

- *Tightrope walking* – with two ropes. This was looking much steadier. Sean's feet were on the rope and he wasn't looking at his feet.

Other observations

Other things Sean's parents said at this review:

We've noticed how much better his swimming is suddenly getting – he's starting to coordinate his arms and legs. His swimming teacher asked, 'What's going on?'

We couldn't believe that he'd won a game of dead lions at a birthday party! Before, Sean would never have been able to lie still for so long. At home, we're noticing that he seems much more settled and not as frustrated with himself. School is doing all the activities too.

Reflection

Great progress was made in that first month – I couldn't hope for anything better. The family remained motivated. They'd done all the activities I'd suggested but had managed to resist the temptation to overcomplicate things. They had stuck to the things I'd asked them to do and were very mindful of the combination of good technique and the activities being fun. It felt as if we now had a reasonable foundation of core strength and some developing proprioceptive functioning to build on.

Elsa's assessment

Like Sean, Elsa was six years old when we met.

Tactile system

- *Feely bag* – Elsa took a long time to warm up but when she was feeling confident she was accurate at discerning single objects. There were no difficulties when I made this harder – she was able to find two objects that were the same (batteries, two bracelets), and find one with each hand.

- *Touch games* – she enjoyed this and had a lovely warm relationship with her parents.

- *Taste games* – she was oversensitive to taste, she found salt and vinegar crisps too tangy. At home, she liked very bland food. She didn't like food she had to chew.

Vestibular system

- *Lying on tummy* – Elsa could lie in a good straight line.

- *Prone extension* – she tried really hard. On her third attempt, she was able to get some elevation when holding her arms in towards her body.

- *Stairs* – the first time of going down she was watching her feet and had both hands on the banister. The second time, I asked her to try one hand on the banister – Elsa did this, watching her feet. The third time, I asked her to try without holding on at all – she was very wobbly and couldn't manage it, feeling very self-conscious, and I noticed how quickly she'd gone from feeling upbeat to being overwhelmed by the enormity of the task.

- *Leaping* – she was doing it really fast. When I asked her to slow down, she was not landing on the cushions or landing then falling off. She didn't want to keep going with this.

Proprioceptive system

- *Commando crawling* – Elsa was wanting to use her legs, and really struggling to move forwards without these. It was slow and effortful.

- *Tightrope walking* – her tiptoe walking was wobbly and she fell off the rope.

- *Stairs* – she came down holding on to one banister, looking at her feet. We worked from here on her not looking at her feet but at me. After five times doing this, she was much more confident and was managing it. We didn't try this with no banister because of how discouraged Elsa had become when we'd tried that earlier.

- *Sitting drawing* – she was very unstable on her chair, sitting cross-legged and very stiff. At one point, she fell off. She moved the page around when she needed to change direction (e.g. to draw the bottom half of the face), and I noticed that her arms were very close to her body as she tried to draw. She held the pencil very tightly. Elsa said that she found writing really hard and that she knew in her head how she wanted the letters to look but they didn't come out that way.

At first glance, Elsa's drawing looks like an easier sort of body to inhabit that Sean's picture. But there's really no body between the head and the legs – just that triangle dress. I was also really struck that her person didn't have any arms or hands, and what her parents and I had observed in the assessment was a really weak shoulder girdle and very little control of anything that she was doing with her hands. It was fascinating to see that mirrored in her picture.

Other observations

Elsa's parents talked about how she was always up and down from her chair when they were trying to eat meals and how often she fell off her chair. We talked about how little sense she had of her body at this stage – not getting those messages from her muscles and joints about position or how much pressure or force to use. I suggested a box for her to put her (bare) feet on that would allow her to sit at the table with a good 90-degree angle between her back and her legs – perhaps with some fluffy/soft material on the box. This was an interim measure while we were trying to build core strength and stability.

Starting programme for the first four weeks

Although some aspects of Elsa's presentation looked very similar to Sean's, the initial programme had a different emphasis. With Elsa, I felt that I was still working to engage her, as she didn't have Sean's enthusiasm for it and seemed overwhelmed by her awareness of the things she couldn't do. I needed to design a programme that was much closer to her current level of functioning and then very gently introduce some challenges that she would manage easily.

It was helpful to have seen from the assessment that Elsa was good at the feely bag game. So although you could argue that she wasn't really needing to practise this because her level of functioning was already good, I thought it would be a good starting point. I wanted something that she felt herself to be good at, that I was confident her parents could make into a fun game, and that doing this would be a good way of introducing the whole idea of games and activities to build those underdeveloped systems.

I'd usually give a child commando crawling to do at the start of a programme, where I wanted to build upper body strength, but I didn't with Elsa, because I thought she was feeling too overwhelmed and discouraged by what she couldn't do. I wanted to find some middle ground – a way of keeping her engaged and building function but without it drawing attention to what she couldn't do. So we did 'feet last', which is fairly quick, quite good fun and hard to fail at. The challenge for the child is to make their feet be the last part of their body to touch the ground when they get out of bed. The first step is for them to turn over on to their tummy and put their hands down on the floor (flat hands, fingers facing forwards). From here they want to support their weight on their hands/straight arms and walk their body as far away from the bed as they can before they put their feet down. The slower they are able to do this, the harder it will be.

Tactile system

- Feely bag.

- Lots of 'mouthly' games, using a straw, making bubbles, blowing and sucking. You'll notice that I did not do taste tests at this stage. I wanted to do things that were fun so that Elsa built an association between these games and a good feeling, and also to do some preparatory work in building strength and stamina.

- Touch games to build bodily awareness and help Elsa feel more comfortable with the sensation of being touched.

Vestibular system

- Lying on tummy.

Proprioceptive system

- *Having bare feet around the house as much as possible* – to increase the amount of sensory input, helping her body to become more aware of itself.

- *Feet last* – coming off the sofa or bed by putting hands on the floor first and 'walking' away from the sofa/bed with as straight a body/arms as possible.

- *No eyes* – because I knew Elsa's family liked going for walks, I suggested that sometimes, when they were on a quiet path, they could take turns to stand in the middle, close their eyes and walk for a few steps with their eyes closed, then open their eyes and see if they were able to stay in a straight line. Asking them to close their eyes when they're doing something very familiar is a very gentle way to begin activities that are forcing the body to get information from the muscles and joints about position and how much pressure or force to use in a movement. It works equally well when eating toast, or something like that, but I didn't want to do that with Elsa because of the difficulties there already were around food and eating.

Review session with parents four weeks after the assessment
Tactile system

- *Feely bag* – Elsa had got even better at these and was able to find really small things and discern different sorts of material. She was delighted with herself that she was better at doing this that either of her parents!

- *Mouthly games* – I could see a difference in strength and stamina as Elsa was progressing to smaller straws and able to use the novelty straws to drink a bit more. She was enjoying doing this and asking for straws if her parents forgot.

Vestibular system

- *Lying on tummy* – she had spent lots of time on her tummy. I noticed from the videos that Elsa was still tending to tuck her arms in close to her body, so we talked about getting her arms out in front of her and noticing her head position.

Proprioceptive system

- *Feet last* – Elsa had become an expert at this and could now get out of bed and off chairs and sofas like this!

- *Commando crawling* – even though I'd thought commando crawling might be too difficult, Elsa's parents had talked to her about this and she was actually really keen to try and do it, so they had come up with a variation called mermaid crawling, which Elsa did with her mermaid costume on. From their video, I could see a huge improvement; she had a good position now, with her arms out in front, her head up, and good action – one arm then the next. It was still effortful but a big improvement in body position and she was beginning to enjoy the challenge.

- *Stairs* – her parents noticed that Elsa was managing the stairs better – she didn't look as precarious as she did – and she was not holding on to her pencil so tightly when she was writing.

- Her mum and dad talked about other things they'd noticed, in particular a big difference with how long Elsa was able to sit at the table. This was really helping with family meals and Elsa eating more. Her parents also noticed that she was not gripping on to her pencil so tightly when she was writing.

Chapter 16

Next Steps in Rebuilding Underdeveloped Vestibular and Proprioceptive Systems

AS you saw from the last chapter, I review progress after about four weeks. This is usually long enough for families to have had a chance to get started and hopefully be seeing some progress, but not so long that the children have completely outgrown the activities.

I really love this review session. As I talked about in Chapter 4, I start working with a number of families at the same time, so that they can be together for the training day and then again for the follow-up groups. The follow-up groups are just for parents or carers – no children this time! Parents and carers can hear about other children and how they're getting on and be able to share ideas, so there's quite a lot to think about, but not so much that it's overwhelming.

I'm always keen to meet parents and carers again and if I've managed to engage families and got the level of challenge right, then, as we could see with Sean and Elsa, they should be beginning to see a difference by now, and that's really exciting to be part of. It is often at this stage that parents or carers are starting to say, 'I don't know if it's a coincidence but...' At other times the difference can be really dramatic. If families have struggled to get started, they can usually still remember the principles of rebuilding underdeveloped systems and it's another chance to get things restarted. Seeing the progress other families have made is a far more powerful incentive to get started than anything I might say. Either way, there's a lot to be aware of and to do at this review point.

First, the big picture: does it seem as if the family have been able to do the games and activities? If they haven't then it's important to understand why. Sometimes it's just that life has been too busy and hard that month (in which case I suggest that they take a break until things get easier again); or maybe there's still work to be done in terms of engagement and the family might be needing more support; or perhaps the challenge has been too hard.

Second, the smaller picture: it's important to get an accurate idea of how often families have been doing the activities. This can feel a little tricky sometimes (especially if they're feeling a bit defensive at not having had as much time as they'd hoped), which is one of the reasons I tend to start working with a number of families at the same time so that I can do the training in a big group and this stage in a smaller group. I find that a group of four or five families works well. In that size of group, one family may have had an unexpectedly stressful or busy month but the others will have managed to get going, and it can be very encouraging for the family who have struggled to get started to hear the progress the others are making. It's also a great way for parents and carers to support each other, sharing ideas about the sorts of adaptations they've been making and any top tips for encouraging their children. It also provides a chance to hear about children at a different stage of development/underdevelopment – again, this can give useful perspective.

If I'm not seeing families as part of that four-stage BUSS programme, I try and ring or email a couple of weeks after the assessment, just to see how they're getting on and to check they've managed to get started. If not, I just push back the date for review, so that they have got a chance to get going.

There are a few general principles I try to stick to when reviewing:

- Don't change the activities a child is doing just because it's the review. If the challenge is right, then stay at that level until there is a shift. It can be challenging for practitioners training in the BUSS model not to feel pressured about coming up with new ideas at this stage of the programme, and to be confident that if the child needs to spend more time consolidating what they're doing, then that's what they need to do.

- Although I've broken things down and talked about splitting the child's body into sections, when I'm doing the review, I encourage families to bring it all back together and look at how the body is functioning as a whole. It is important not to assume, for example, that a child being better at commando crawling means that their body is now working as a synchronized unit. It's about looking at the big picture and noticing if, for example, a child is still very heavy footed as they come down some stairs, or their arms still look as if they have a life of their own when they're jumping. Both of these would suggest to me that the child still needs to do lots of floor-based work to get the body working as an integrated whole unit.

Assuming things have got started, then it's at this review point that I want to help families focus in on *technique*, so that their child can get the maximum benefit from the things they're doing.

Commando crawling is a good example of this. Often to start with, we just want to get children doing it: getting used to being in this position and beginning to move themselves forwards. Usually, if they've practised, they'll be a lot better after four weeks (we saw that with Elsa and Sean). And it's at this point that I want parents and carers to notice all those things we talked about in the assessment:

- What is the head position like?

- Is the child looking down at the floor?

- Is the child looking where they're going?

- Notice the arms. Are they down by their sides? Are they pushing themselves forwards? Are both arms working together or have they got the 'alternating arms' technique going?

- Then the hips and legs. Where is the power for the movement coming from? Are the hips in contact with the floor? Are the legs still and straight?

Some of this will depend on the child's starting point, but wherever they are, there will usually be something about technique that could make it more effective. And here it's important to help parents and carers notice what's happening so that they can be thinking of how to improve things. So if a child is commando crawling with their head down, then instead of suggesting to parents and carers that they tell the child to look up, I want them to get the child's attention and make it more fun to be looking up than looking at the floor. This stops it feeling so much like an exercise and more like a game. With older teenagers, I find that it's helpful to get them into the way of checking their technique along with their parents and carers, using a mirror or making a recording of them doing it and then analyzing it together.

So, being mindful of the enormous effort the whole family will have put into the amount of progress the child has made, I want to be hugely encouraging of what they've done and at the same time, quite picky about technique!

Next steps

I'm hoping that by this stage you will have a feel for how the BUSS model starts rebuilding underdeveloped systems. There are a lot of options for where it's possible to go from there, but it's not a formula that can be rolled out and applied to all children whose systems are underdeveloped, and I don't think it's helpful to pretend that it's easier than it is! The next stage will vary from child to child and usually evolves within the partnership between a practitioner and a family.

To give you an idea of what an intervention might look like from here, we'll follow on with some of the children and families you've already met. Let's start with Sean and Elsa.

Sean

Given how well things had gone in the first four weeks, my challenge was to keep the momentum going, changing the activities enough to keep them stimulating and interesting, but not so much that we lost that good attention to technique and helping to keep Sean in the moment of what we were doing.

Next steps in building foundation systems
Tactile system

- *Bringing together straw games and vestibular system games* – playing straw games on the floor.

Vestibular system

- *Moving from prone extension into Batman driving* – I'm told by someone, who sounded very sure about it, that there is a Batman film where Batman drives the Batmobile by lying on his tummy (I'm hoping this is right!). For this, the child starts in the prone extension position but with feet tucked under the sofa and holding something to be a 'steering wheel' in their outstretched hands (a dinner plate works well). The idea is that the child then 'corners', leaning over to one side then coming back into the middle before leaning over to the other side. This is really tricky, so to begin with we just tried one or two 'corners'; but as Sean got better at it, we made the course harder, until Sean could 'drive' from home to his granny's.

Proprioceptive system

- *Commando crawling* – with parents doing activities that were really encouraging Sean to have his head looking forwards rather than down.

- *Tightrope walking* – making a beam off the ground. Sean's family used a piece of decking plank and put a couple of bricks under each end. Raising the beam off the ground meant that this became a helpful activity for his vestibular system too.

- *Bunny hops* – on the ground and side to side across the beam. With bunny hopping, it's important to make sure that the child's feet are together and that the movement has two distinct elements to it: first, that the hands touch down (flat hands, fingers facing forwards); then the feet follow, landing with feet together. It's good if the knees can be together too but it's not a deal breaker. I use the 'magic glue' that always lives in my pocket to stick those feet together before they start. I always emphasize feet together for take-off and landing.

  When a child's shoulder girdle isn't very strong and their legs are, they can often overshoot this kind of movement and so it's worth taking some time to get the technique right. I find that it's easiest if the child starts in a crouched position with their bottom on their heels, and moves forwards by stretching their arms forwards and putting both hands on the floor in front of them and then jumping their legs in behind them. When they land, their feet should be together. Because I want to build the child's shoulder girdle and get them used to taking their weight through their shoulders down straight arms to their hands, I tend to emphasize that first bit of the movement, encouraging them to slap their hands down on the floor so they make a big noise as they hit the floor. Like Sean, they might need quite a bit of coaching to begin with to get both the rhythm and the pace right. When he had got really good at this (able to do it accurately and quickly without having to think too much about it), he was able to move on to doing this along the beam.

  Once he was able to do that, we introduced bunny hopping from side to side across the beam – that is a hard challenge and one we're still working on!

Reassessment eight weeks after first assessment
Tactile system

- *Feely bag* – what a difference! Sean was much slower and more thoughtful, taking his time, and much more accurate. He was able to manage the challenge of finding two objects and was significantly less frenetic as he was doing this. He told me that my feely bag was a bit too easy for him – and this time he was right!

- *Straw games* – he was still really enjoying doing these; making bubble mountains, drinking milkshakes and now even managing jelly through a straw.

Vestibular system

- *Lying on tummy* – Sean could do this in a beautiful straight line, with a great head position, and no wriggling or squirming.

- *Prone extension* – he could do this in a good straight line, holding with good elevation (but could probably get this higher).

- *Leaping* – he landed cleanly on each cushion. His mum has worked out lots of ways to help him slow down and has coached him through these.

- *Stairs* – he did these one foot at a time without holding the banister (although it looked as if he still had to concentrate quite hard on that!), but to see his delight at being so much better than when we met two months ago was so good.

Proprioceptive system

- *Commando crawling* – he was so much stronger and was confidently and competently doing about ten 'steps' without using his legs (again, I thought there was still room to grow here – he was tiring quite quickly).

- *Sitting drawing* – he had his feet on the ground and was getting all the stability from his core. Sean himself noticed that he wasn't pressing down nearly as hard with his pencil. And what a brilliant drawing it was! Sean is slaying a dragon in the picture, and it was such a delight to watch him drawing this (adding more detail than had been asked for) but most of all, seeing a body that looked as if fun, play and adventure might be possible in it – such a shift from that first picture.

Other observations
Sean's parents said:

> At home, we've noticed such a difference in Sean's confidence and how cheerful he is. We're beginning to see a lovely sense of humour developing that we've never seen before.

Feedback from school was also very positive. Sean's teacher said, at parents' evening, that she couldn't believe the difference in him. She said it was really noticeable in PE and when he was writing too. In PE, he was more coordinated and stable. He was actually able to take part in a sporting tournament, which requires coordination. When he wrote, he was not pressing down as hard either. His writing was smaller and more readable. The difference from the beginning of the school year was very noticeable. He was also not just scribbling but actually managing to draw decent shapes. His drama therapist also said that he was now telling stories with a beginning, middle and end.

Reflection

It always feels such a privilege to have been instrumental in helping to support a child like Sean in taking such a huge leap forwards in terms of his foundation systems. It was really exciting to see how his confidence and sense of himself was developing, and to watch family relationships grow at the same time. I wanted to continue to work with Sean's family for longer because, although there had been great improvement, I thought that we could get much further. Seeing how quickly he still tired made me think that we could continue to build vestibular functioning. There was also still work to do in the proprioceptive system so that he wasn't using his eyes to track movement (he was still doing this from time to time). And although Sean was able to stay in the moment of an experience and manage the uncertainty of not knowing for longer, this still needed a lot of scaffolding and support from parents at home and adults at school. Therefore, I wanted us to keep using the BUSS model to try and keep things moving forwards.

From this eight-week review, I could conclude that the programme Sean was following was still at the right level, so it was just a case of talking the family through aspects of technique to be honing in on, and thinking of ways to make obstacle races and challenges so that Sean continued to feel excited about doing the activities.

It was great that Sean's parents were able to bring him to the BUSS gym club I run and so we were able to continue to build those foundation systems. And I can tell you that he is doing brilliantly!

Elsa

I love it when I'm surprised at that four-week review with just how much progress a child and family have made since the start of the programme. I hadn't expected that with Elsa. Knowing now how skilled her parents were at getting the level of challenge just right for her (which included knowing exactly when to suggest they do something), I felt confident to give a wider range of activities for the next month.

Next steps in building foundation systems
Tactile system

- *Straw games* – we combined straw games with tummy time and made the drinks thicker, aiming for a yogurt within a couple of weeks.

- *Feely bags* – we moved on to games that involved the upper and lower body, like the giant jigsaw game.

Vestibular system

- *Lying on tummy* – now that Elsa was used to being on her tummy and able to get into a good position, I wanted her to stay in the position for longer and to do more from this position. Therefore, it needed to get a bit more interesting – this is where it can be really helpful to move some of the tactile games onto the floor and play them as part of tummy time. For Elsa, we had to make this very enticing to start with, and the family played a game that had three small bowls in a line in front of them on the floor. The middle bowl had a mix of either milk and white chocolate buttons or green and red grapes in it. The challenge for Elsa was to use her straw to suck each one up and sort them into the different bowls, so by the end there was nothing left in the middle bowl, and the other two bowls had the same colour chocolate or grapes in them. She really enjoyed this and it helped to build that association of being on her tummy on the floor and having fun.

   The family didn't have to keep using 'sweeteners' and soon they were lying on their tummies and blowing bubbles, feathers, balls and cars to each other. Elsa's family found that they could also make the games a bit longer and more complicated – for example, playing snakes and ladders or noughts and crosses lying on their tummies, using straws to move the counters.

- *Prone extension* – we untucked Elsa's feet from under the sofa so that she could lift her arms and feet up at the same time. I also gave her parents the information about Batman driving so that they knew the next stage of things to move on to.

- *Stepping stones* – To make this more challenging, I wanted to introduce some changes of direction, so asked the family to make two rows of cushions instead of one. This meant that Elsa could jump sideways and diagonally, as well as forwards and backwards. Elsa and mum made up a great game, where mum would give the instructions and Elsa had to try and follow them. So mum might say, 'jump forward for three cushions…now jump across to the cushion on your right… now jump backwards for two cushions…' to make it more challenging as Elsa's level of skill increased.

Proprioceptive system

- *Mermaid crawling* – Elsa'a parents had set up a great obstacle course where Elsa was commando crawling along the floor, then using her arms to pull herself up onto a small footstool and from there onto the sofa, then; commando crawling along the sofa and coming off the end by putting her hands down and walking her body as far away from the sofa as she could before she let her legs come down. Fantastic! When families are doing as well as this, I feel my job is to not to get in the way – this was far more interesting than the commando crawling I'd been suggesting!

- *Tightrope walking* – I suggested they reintroduced this now, but starting with two ropes, feet about hip-distance apart, with Elsa doing bear walks, jumping and walking forwards and backwards. They needed to focus on heel strike/toe peel and playing games to encourage Elsa to keep her head up (she'd been a tiptoe walker in the assessment).

- *Bunny hops* – emphasizing the hand slap part of the movement and getting both feet jumping together.

Reassessment eight weeks after first assessment
Tactile system

- *Feely bag* – Elsa showed great discrimination and was more relaxed and much more confident. She wanted me to challenge her and make it harder.

Vestibular system

- *Drawing* – Elsa was able to sit at the table and draw. She had a lovely stable position, with stability coming from her core, no sense of her being precarious, no falling off her chair – and she produced a completely different sort of picture of herself! It was lovely to watch Elsa do this picture, and to see the detail that she was adding (those circles!) and compare it to the little girl who had fallen off her chair as she tried to draw that first picture. And of course, to see those arms and hands was just fantastic!

- *Prone extension* – Elsa was making good progress with elevation and stamina. After two weeks, her parents reported that she had been able to hold a good position for five seconds, and after four weeks, for ten seconds. Elsa was delighted with herself and so excited to show me how well she could do this now. They were just beginning to try Batman driving at home.

- *Stepping stones* – this was becoming much more controlled. Elsa was able to slow things down, not falling off as much but still losing a bit of core stability at times when she was jumping backwards.

- *Stairs* – she was not holding on to the banister or looking at her feet. She still occasionally looked a bit wobbly but there was a huge improvement.

- *Bunny hops* – again there was a big improvement here but when Elsa's feet were off the ground she got much wobblier all over.

Proprioceptive system

- *Commando (mermaid) crawling* – Elsa was still holding that good position, building strength and stamina and able to keep going for much longer. She looked so much more in control of her body and it was working as one unit in a way that it just couldn't before.

- *Tightrope walking* – she was looking nice and steady on two ropes. We tried again with one rope and I could see how much better Elsa's core stability and body awareness were – she able to walk along the rope slowly, maintained good posture and control and wasn't tiptoe walking.

Next steps – plan for the next four weeks
Tactile system

- Continue to build discriminatory functioning. We also talked about starting to do some tactile play, like outdoor hand and foot painting (I find wallpaper lining paper is great for this), games like mud kitchens, walking in wet sand (maybe something for holiday time!), making dough (from the wet stage through to kneading) and all sorts of games that are quite messy and allow for expression and exploration.

Vestibular system

- Continue with all tummy time games.

- *Leaping from cushion to cushion* – keep practising this and increase the difficulty as Elsa gets better at it. And when she's really stable we can think about two lines of cushions and zig zagging across – but we're a long way from there just now.

Proprioceptive system

- *Commando crawling* – continue to encourage Elsa to crawl over obstacles (like cushions) and pull herself up onto the sofa as well as doing the feet last to get off. We talked about the 'lever point' and could see the point at which Elsa's body started to wobble when she was holding this in the 'as far away from the sofa as you can walk your hands' position. It would be good to get her to stop just before that point and see how long she could hold it for – up to about ten seconds.

- *Tightrope walking* – move on to one rope again, just going through the same sequence: forwards, back, then turning, and with obstacles.

- *Bunny hopping* – her parents had bought a beam on the internet so Elsa was going to try all of the tightrope activities on this.

Reflection

Although Elsa had a slower start than Sean, as you can see, she was making fantastic progress. Her mum was keeping a log of the changes she had noticed that happened during the intervention and in the year that followed (see Chapter 17).

Also in Chapter 17, Nadia, Lenny and Amber's parents talk about their progression in the BUSS model, going through the stages from assessment to the end of the programme. I thought it might be helpful now to just 'catch up' with a few of the other children I've talked about in the book so that you have an overview of the whole programme.

There are some children, like Janey (Chapter 5), and Sami (Chapter 12), who I only saw a couple of times – by shifting one part of the system, other things fell into place and the parents felt confident about moving forwards on their own. With other children, it's helpful to stay involved for a bit longer.

LEROY: NEXT STEPS IN BUILDING FOUNDATION SYSTEMS

You might remember Leroy, who I talked about in Chapters 2 and 5. Leroy's carer had come to the BUSS training day but hadn't been able to be part of the rest of the programme, so I'd seen them at home instead.

The initial focus of the work was on building oral strength and stamina and encouraging Leroy to lie on his tummy and start commando crawling. When I went back to visit a few weeks after the assessment, life had been very challenging for Leroy's foster carer and it had been hard to keep doing the activities. We thought about ways to keep it interesting and that would fit quite easily into the routine of the day – reading books like *The Gruffalo* (Donaldson 2017) or *Dear Zoo* (Campbell 2010) and then pretending to be the different animals – slithering along like the snake and stomping around like the elephant can make it more fun without increasing the complexity of the activity.

I kept seeing Leroy over the next few months, and we moved on from commando crawling to regular crawling, then bear walking, bunny hopping and being all sorts of different animals that involved being on our hands and knees! It was lovely to watch him be able to move around and play in the garden without falling over or bumping into things. He was now able to use his arms and upper body as an integral part of his movements, rather than leading with his legs for everything. At nursery, he wasn't getting as frustrated because he was able to do the things he was trying to do, such as pour sand into his bucket. His oral strength improved really quickly and soon he was able to eat a whole sandwich and actually seemed to taste what he was eating. Leroy is waiting for an adoptive family and I'm hoping to be able to follow things through with them when he moves on.

Chapter 17

Over to Parents: Reflections on Experiences of Using the BUSS Model from Lenny, Amber, Nadia, Elsa and Percy

I AM very grateful to the foster carers and adoptive parents who were happy for me to talk about their experiences of using this model throughout the book. I wanted this chapter to be for them to talk about things in their own words. What follows are five different accounts of using the model, from the parents and carers of Lenny, Amber, Nadia, Elsa and Percy. Some are presented as the transcripts of interviews, others are parents' and foster carers' own writing. I hope you find them as useful as I have!

Lenny

Lenny's mum came on the first training I did in Leeds when we'd moved here. She came with school and from there we started to do some work together. Lenny has been coming to gym club from the very first session back in 2016 and it is lovely to have been able to stay in touch with the family. I met with Lenny's mum to talk about her experiences of this way of working – she has a lot of experience of it!

Background

Me: So, your wee boy is Lenny, and Lenny is now seven years old.

Mum: Yes, and he was five when we first met you.

Me: And can you tell us a bit about Lenny.

Mum: Things were really tough when we met you. He was really hyperaroused. He would run around and not be able to regulate himself. No spatial awareness, he would just run through other children and hit out and lash out; he just couldn't contain himself very well. He really struggled at home and at school.

Assessment

We whizzed through all the activities at top speed – probably the fastest assessment I've done! Because I'd already had a glimpse of Lenny at school, and from speaking to his mother, we agreed it would work better to do the active parts of the vestibular and proprioceptive system where we were on the floor, before addressing the tactile system, which involved more sitting down.

Vestibular system

Lenny struggled to hold himself in a straight line on his tummy, and when I asked him to come up into prone extension, he just flipped onto his back – he couldn't hold that position.

Proprioceptive system

Commando crawling was really slow and effortful and very quickly Lenny resorted to using his legs to move himself forwards.

Going down the stairs, Lenny was like a little rocket, but when he slowed down we could see that he was really wobbly and needed to use his eyes to track his feet. This picture of Lenny having no real idea where his body was if he wasn't using his eyes to track his movements (so not getting the messages about position or how much pressure or force to use in a movement from the muscles and joints inside his body) fitted with what I'd seen at school of him crashing into/through other children and into tables as he was moving about the classroom.

Tactile system

Lenny couldn't manage not knowing what was in the feely bag and just grabbed it from me, so the assessment at that early stage was about not being able to stay in the moment of the experience and manage both the uncertainty of not knowing and of not being in charge. I was not able to get a clear idea about discriminatory functioning.

Me: We did some drawing and it was a whole-arm/whole-body movement. Lenny was gouging his way through the page – you could see he had lots of ideas and was getting more and more frustrated at not being able to get them down.

Mum: Yes, the fine motor control was really poor and the cause of so many tantrums and frustrations at home.

Me: It was interesting because Lenny was this mix of getting really frustrated with himself when he couldn't do something, but then being able to tolerate us being quite fussy about technique and really wanting to get it right.

Mum: Yes, he'd keep going because he really wanted to achieve and do well.

Plan

Vestibular system

With tummy time, the first aim was to try and get Lenny into a straight line, with his parents lying on either side of him when they were doing a story at night, just to encourage his body into a good straight position.

Mum: He really got to like that, and we quickly shifted from having to read only the shortest of stories to being able to make the stories longer and longer as he got more used to the position. It got so we could read whole chapters of quite interesting books, rather than having to fly through picture books. Once he was good at this, we brought out the gym ball, and he really liked that. At first, we held him so he was steady on the ball and then he was able to start walking forwards on the ball – he really enjoyed that – and you could see his shoulder strength building.

Me: By that time his core strength was really developing, wasn't it? He could hold a nice straight line on the ball, and he was into wanting to 'control' his body on the ball.

Mum: Yes, he loved the challenge of this and even if we only had a few minutes he'd want us to be doing it, seeing if he was getting any better at it.

Me: The other thing you did to build that vestibular system was to use a hammock you had, and Lenny would lie across the hammock on his tummy, just gently swaying!

Mum: That was very calming for him and we'd use it lots of times during the day. It worked best if we could spot the moment before things started to get difficult and to put some music on while he was lying in there, just for a few minutes, to calm things right down again.

Proprioceptive system – crawling and commando crawling

Mum: He found this so hard and we had to do lots of different things to try and keep him on task. For Lenny, crawling through a pop-up tunnel (towards chocolate buttons) was a good incentive, or just trying to do short bursts – so to begin with maybe only three or four 'steps' of commando crawling, making sure that Lenny was using his shoulders rather than his knees. We played lots of games of pretending to be tortoises, where I'd put a heavy cushion on Lenny's back, to try and keep his legs still and make sure it was his arms doing the work. Or I'd hold his feet, pretending to be giving him a turbo boost, but really just to try and keep his legs still.

Tactile system

Here we were trying to recalibrate that limbic system, hoping to get some time when Lenny wasn't in a fight or flight state of mind, but also trying to encourage some discriminatory functioning too.

Mum: To begin with we did the feely bags, and he really enjoyed those. We started with five objects and then moved on to having two bags with the same objects in each bag – this was very good for just keeping him on a game for longer; and because we were doing it so often, it was much easier for him to see that if he didn't win every time, it wasn't the end of the world. He really liked the taste tests – and we did lots of blowing and sucking – and the bubble mountains (we still do them if I think that he's wobbling or just to reconnect with some of these things); we did lots of blowing bubbles in glasses, and blow football – definitely a winner!

Me: I was very impressed with how good you were at grading things, not necessarily moving from one thing to the next but pacing it so well.

Mum: I found I had to 'read' Lenny each day – how he was feeling, what else had been happening and what I thought he was going to manage. I wanted him to succeed rather than set him up to fail!

Me: So much of the time you were using the tactile system things to try and look at the emotional side of things.

Mum: Yes, all the time – and people began to notice a difference. At school, staff were saying that Lenny had really calmed down a lot, and it was nice just to have people saying something positive to you, rather than doing the walk of shame. He managed to tolerate groups after school, which he had not been able to do before, and extracurricular activities he'd not managed before – it was really life-changing for him.

Me: I remember you noticing his frustration tolerance shifting.

Mum: The whole queuing up and taking turns was a big no-no right back at the beginning, but I remember we went to a farm about a year or so after we'd met you, and, normally, going to a farm and having to wait for a go on a rope swing would be really hard for him. I was a bit anxious watching him queue up, and it was a bit of a free for all, nobody was really supervising their children and he stood and waited and waited. I was thinking, oh gosh, something's going to happen in a minute, but he just waited and then he said to a girl, 'Can I have a go please?' I was amazed that he could manage that! So that was – wow – that was a major step. Then he's moved on to other successes with his football; he's a goalie and was scouted by a premiership team and went and trained with them for a while – and managed it! He really enjoyed that – he's doing so well.

Me: It's great to see, isn't it? I see him each week at gym club and it's been fantastic to see how he's come on. I remember to begin with we only had four children (and three coaches) but still it felt so chaotic! I remember them jumping into the foam pit and trying to crawl across on their tummies but their vestibular systems were so underdeveloped, they flipped over onto their backs and were unable to right themselves.

Mum: They have come on so far. They power through that foam pit now!

Me: Yes, really straight bodies – heads up, arms down! But gym club is just the icing on the cake. It's that day-in, day-out work that you've done at home that makes the difference. You manage so well to build these things into everyday life so that it isn't a huge chore each time to do them.

Mum: It really isn't, just ten minutes here and there – we fit it in, as and when. I remember one time being on holiday and noticing Lenny was getting a bit hyper so we found a wall and as a whole family we did wall squats!

Me: Brilliant! To settle that central nervous system down.

Mum: Yes, and it is just repetition, repetition, repetition. It worked for us!

A SWAYING KIND OF ROCK

If a family have got a hammock, it can be really helpful in rebuilding an underdeveloped vestibular system. I don't normally suggest families go and buy a hammock at the beginning of this intervention, because usually it's possible to use floor-time activities to build core strength well enough. But there are occasions when a child's core stability is so underdeveloped that they need more than this. In my experience, this is usually children who have been affected by alcohol use in the womb, and who have a heaviness about their movement that seems to emanate from their core rather than the 'stompy' heaviness of an underdeveloped proprioceptive system. They often seem so floppy that they can't hold themselves up, or move themselves around easily. If they get stuck in one position (usually on their tummy) they seem to find it really hard to push themselves back up.

If, after a month of lots of work to build core stability through tummy time, things aren't significantly different, it can be helpful to think about a hammock or, if it's easier or more practical, a rocking chair.

The advantage of a hammock is that it's easier to get a gentle swaying motion than it is with something like a swing, and the child can be lying on their tummy. There's also something very containing about being in a hammock.

With younger children, the best way to start is if the parent or carer lies in the hammock on their back and the child lies on top of them on their tummy, and they gently sway together, even if it's just for a few moments.

Amber

When I met Amber and her family, she was 14 and was the oldest child I'd worked with. I wasn't hugely confident that I'd be able to make a difference, as she'd already seen a lot of specialists and had a lot of different therapies. I'm so pleased not only that I was wrong, but that I had the chance to work with Amber and her family because it really helped to shape the model and this way of working. I'll always be hugely grateful to them for that.

Here is a transcript of an interview I did with Amber's mum a few months after we'd finished what was a three-session intervention.

Background
Me: Tell us a bit about Amber.

Mum: We met Amber when she was four and she came to live with us. She was a very bright, loving, excitable child, but from the very first time we met her, we noticed that she was quite awkward in her movements; things seemed quite jerky and she was quite awkward moving about. She would often 'root' herself, very keen to be sitting down doing things rather than running round, and she had a very distinct tremor in her hands. The tremor had been noticed before but was thought to be anxiety related and so it would settle down in time.

When Amber first came to live with us we did lots of early learning type things; she spent ages playing in water, [making] handprints, blowing bubbles, playing in the sand, all of that sort of thing, trying to see what she was interested in, rather than things that children her age might have been doing. She certainly wasn't interested in anything like pencils.

As she got older, the tremor continued. Getting dressed in the mornings was really hard; she needed to cling on to my arms to steady herself as she tried to put things on, or she'd be rooted to her bed to try and get things on herself.

Me: So she was not able to balance herself at all?

Mum: No, and eating something like breakfast always took ages. It was all so laborious for her. I noticed how conscious she was of what she couldn't do, right from an early age.

Me: When I met Amber she was 14, and it sounds as if things weren't very different.

Mum: On a bodily level, no, not at all. She was still going down the stairs holding on to the banister, with two feet on each step and looking at what she was doing. Despite this, she wanted to get her own breakfast and be independent but the attention she had to pay, opening the box, pouring it into the bowl, all took ages, and we were having to allow so much time for things and for her to feel independent.

Me: It must have been frustrating for Amber.

Mum: Yes, so she just spent most of the time with a kind of frown on her face and her head down. There was a time we had to deal with, just before we met you, when school were in touch with us saying that they thought she was showing signs of aggression, because she'd sit with her fist clenched, her arms by her sides and a kind of frown on her face. It just felt as if everything was such an effort for her.

Me: And Amber talked about how tired she was.

Mum: Yes, she'd get in from school and just sit or lie on her bed. She never wanted to do any clubs or activities. Sometimes I'd suggest that we might do something together and she'd start to say 'yes' and you could see that on some level she wanted to do it, but then she'd sigh and say, 'Maybe later'. She would be exhausted by the end of the day and would need to go to bed quite early for her age. So she was spending more and more time in her room, withdrawn from everything.

And it has also had such an impact on her confidence and relationships.

Even in Year 1 she was moving herself away from the other children because she didn't want them to see what she couldn't do, saying that she was different from them. She would go to extreme lengths to avoid doing any written work; you could see that she had lots of ideas and she'd want to tell you about them but she just couldn't write them down – it was just all too much.

Me: And when she did write?

Mum: It just seemed as if she could never get into a comfortable position. We tried so many things – what height her chair should be, where the page should be, every single pencil grip under the sun. And you could see how tense she was with the effort. All the focus of her effort was on the making of the mark on the page, which didn't leave anything left for the thoughts – so by the time she'd got round to the writing she couldn't remember what she was wanting to say.

Her confidence plummeted and we could see her world narrowing.

Neurologists got involved, and she had MRI (magnetic resonance imaging) scans for the tremor. She had been seen by occupational therapists, educational psychologists and CAMHS, and people seemed concerned about how tense and uncomfortable she was in her own body.

And all the time the years were passing and that gap between Amber and her peers was getting wider and wider. By the time she was at secondary school she made all her choices about subjects based on which required the least amount of writing – which was such a shame; she was so interested in history, but there was just too much writing in the exams. Although school had agreed to arrange a scribe for exams, the day-to-day writing and note-taking in lessons were impossible for her. On and on this seemed to go, being re-referred to specialists she'd seen before who said, 'Oh, it's just the same' but didn't have any answers. Amber herself got more and more low and she saw herself become more and more different from her peers.

Me: So by the time you met me you must have been thinking, 'Oh no, not another person who's going to tell us what to do.'

Mum: Well, yes, but we've always given everything a try so we thought we would try this. But honestly after ten years of people saying you should do this, try this, we were feeling rather despondent. So I really didn't expect anything major.

Assessment

Me: I came and noticed exactly what you said – Amber was upstairs when I arrived and she came down, gripping the banister with both hands, two feet on each step and being so cautious. She almost seemed slowed up in everything; in her speech, her thinking, how she was doing things; she just embodied her physical state. It was so hard to see and I remember thinking that if she could have had an invisibility cloak then that would have been perfect for her.

And then when I was talking to her about the ideas of systems being underdeveloped, she really came alive – she completely understood.

When we did the assessment, I could see how Amber struggled even to get her body into a straight line when she was lying on the floor. She couldn't get up into the prone extension at all and wasn't able to take even a 'step' with commando crawling. We used a gym ball and she was so wobbly and couldn't get her hands flat on the floor or use straight arms to support herself.

Plan

We agreed that all three systems were underdeveloped and we worked on all three, as follows:

Tactile system

Taste tests and feely bags.

Vestibular system

Tummy time, prone extension (starting with feet tucked under the sofa to get into a straight line), lying on her tummy across (rather than the normal up and down way) a hammock, just very gently swaying while she watched her iPad.

Proprioceptive system

Feet last, commando crawling, doing things with eyes closed.

Me: How was it for you doing all of those activities?

Mum: It was a really nice way of connecting, regularly, throughout the day (we were doing the exercises five or six times a day). We always knew they were just short slots – I'd say to start with, 'Let's just do ten minutes', but then we'd often be having fun with them and end up doing 20 minutes. Literally within that first week we were noticing a change – she could get her body into a straight line by herself and no longer needed the sofa. In prone extension, she was gradually able to see more and more of the bookcase that was in front of her.

I think the fact that even within a week we saw that difference spurred us on. I noticed straightaway that the way she responded was different. Before, when I'd ask if she wanted to do something, she'd look as if she did but it always looked as if it was such an effort. Amber would say, 'Maybe later' and we'd rarely end up doing it. Now when I was asking her to do these games she'd just say yes and we'd get started and we almost always had fun.

Me: You were great at thinking about that next stage ahead, keeping the challenge going a little bit at a time.

Mum: Well it was funny, I think we were both so astonished at how quickly she was making progress that we'd have to think, 'Oh, what shall we do now? Let's try and get even higher/further.' So we had a lot of fun. When she was lifting herself up in prone extension we had to keep thinking of things further up the wall that she could see!

Me: When we'd done that together, Amber's head wasn't even coming up off the floor.

Review

I came back two weeks later and was delighted with Amber's progress. She was upstairs when I arrived and she walked down, looking at me, not holding on to the banister and with one foot on each step.

Mum: She was so pleased to show you all that she could do. It was such an amazing difference.

Me: So we made everything much harder. It was amazing to see just how quickly that vestibular system had developed – lovely core stability and a confidence when her feet were off the ground. I wanted us to work a bit more on that, but also to focus on building up shoulder girdle strength and getting her body working as a coherent unit.

Next steps in building foundation systems
Tactile system
Advanced level feely bags and taste tests.

Vestibular system
Prone extension became Batman driving, and we introduced things like jumping and stepping stones, with Amber's feet off the ground.

Proprioceptive system

Amber's mum devised a brilliant thing with bands and hoops to keep that shoulder girdle going, as well as crawling and commando crawling. And Amber stayed really motivated and engaged – her parents kept making it all such good fun.

Mum: I think she was so warmed by you noticing the difference – she'd had years of seeing professionals and nothing changing and here she was, every day, finding she could do more and more things. It got to the point that nearly everything we were doing in the house we were thinking, 'Oh we could turn this into a taste test, or a feely bag challenge.' She was able to progress on to them so quickly – as well as writing on her back and the shapes. I couldn't believe how quickly she got a good sense of that.

The feely bags were good because at the beginning we had lots of different objects, then the same set of things in two bags, but she very quickly moved on to the fabric feely bags.

Me: I came back two weeks later and again noticed a huge improvement – you describe it better than I do.

How are things now?

Mum: Everything is just smoother, less jerky, more controlled, and Amber is moving about more and seems to be getting pleasure in moving about. She'll come down frequently throughout the day, in the evening and at the weekend, just to get things, to do things and is suggesting that we do things together – or make something. She just seems comfortable in her body and as if she can do the things that she wants to do. It is just a lot smoother – she is less tired, she has energy to do things, she is calm and gentle, comfortable in herself.

Me: And the shakiness and the tremor?

Mum: No, I haven't seen it. In fact, she's started writing me little notes and messages. And the tremor is hardly there at all. Her face has just relaxed – she laughs and we see the humour that we saw in her all those years ago, that slightly mischievous girl who was always there but it felt as if it was all just weighted down by her body. But now it really does feel as if something's been lifted. She attempts things, she enjoys things. It's as if she feels right in her own body now. Just utterly different.

School have noticed a difference too – they said that she's interacting more, not looking worried about everything, joking, having a laugh. She's moved away from that thing of wanting to be invisible to actually wanting to be there and be noticed and not be invisible.

She's made a friend and they've even been swimming together.

Me: Fantastic! She'd never have enjoyed that before.

Mum: We took her swimming many times over the years and it was never something she was that keen to do – she enjoyed it when she was in the water, but it was always such a chore and so laborious having to get changed, take her clothes off, put her costume on, then swim, then do it all again. But she arranged it herself and they got the bus there and back and had a brilliant time. She is talking about joining clubs and things – the climbing club at school – all sorts of things.

Me: It's great! And we had a wee chat with Amber just before we sat down to talk together and she described herself as happier, calmer and more confident. She didn't mention the movement stuff, but just her sense of herself having shifted.

Mum: It's as if that weight has been taken off her and she's just able to move.

Me: You did it all so well, and you did such a great job at keeping it interesting.

Mum: The other thing that utterly amazes me is that we spent ten years going round and round seeing different people, and I'm astonished that at her age we could still make a difference, and so quickly – all in six weeks. We continue to do the exercises, but less frequently or intensely. We get the sense that Amber needs to keep 'topping up' work on these systems, maybe because she came to it at an older age, but each time we have another few sessions, the benefits return.

Nadia

Nadia and her family were one of the first families that I worked with on the four-stage training, assessment and intervention model. I met with her mum a couple of months after the intervention was complete to reflect on things.

Me: What was your experience of this intervention?

Mum: Well, we came on the course and heard all about it, then got the programme. And we were quite surprised by some of the things that were on there.

Me: What sort of things?

Mum: You said that when she sat she was a bit floppy but we'd never noticed that – because she's physically quite strong we didn't think there was any issue with her shoulder girdle. She climbs and does other things so we thought that would all be fine.

Me: I noticed that she was just so determined and that carried her through so many things.

Mum: Yes, if you say something is a challenge, she absolutely takes it on. So we were quite surprised. And we were thinking that our issue with Nadia was her managing her emotions so how can thinking about her shoulder strength help with that!

Assessment

From the *tactile system* aspect of the assessment we could see that Nadia was using her eyes a lot to help her find things in the feely bag. She was wanting to rush everything and struggled to stay with what we were doing in the moment, wanting to be on to the next thing all the time. As regards the *vestibular system*, Nadia was able to get into a nice straight line on her tummy but not able to lift herself up into the prone extension position. We noticed that she was needing to hold on and was quite jerky in her movements. From the *proprioceptive* part of the assessment we could see that commando crawling was very slow and effortful, and when she was coming down the stairs she was really slamming her feet down on them. Her mum had noticed that on school days Nadia was filling her shoes with little stones and she said that this was to help her feel her feet. On the tightrope, Nadia struggled to stay on the rope, tending to compensate for this by going really fast. When we slowed her down, we could see how unstable she was in the middle and how reliant she was on her eyes to track her feet.

Plan
Tactile system

- Feely bags, straw games, lots of touch games on Nadia's feet (foot printing, scrunching things, games in the sand) and taste games.

Vestibular system

- Tummy time, prone extension and lying across the gym ball.

Proprioceptive system

- Commando crawling, bunny hopping, bear walking, wall presses, tightrope walking.

How did you get on?
Tactile system

Mum: She loved the feely bag – we still do that, even though she's really good at it. She got really good at all of the touch games – she loves playing the drawing on her back game. We did lots of the straw things but she's kind of grown out of those now, and lots of the games with her feet, which she really enjoyed.

Vestibular system

Mum: We didn't do as much on her tummy as we should have, but she really loved the ball and that was good because it really exposed her weaknesses so we could see when she was getting better at it.

Proprioceptive system

Mum: We started with commando crawling and she was quite slow at first – but to be honest, the first time we saw her do it, we thought she was great at it! It was really only when she had one of her friends round and they were both doing the things that we could see what a difference there was between her and her friend. And now we see her and it's just incredible. The difference is amazing.

What did you notice?

Me: Tell us about the difference.

Mum: After a couple of weeks, I started to notice a slight difference. She was better on the ball, I thought. And then she had a friend round for tea, and he wasn't sharing as much as she thought he should be. Instead of screaming at him, she said, 'Mummy, he's not doing it.' I said, 'Oh, will you do it?' and he did, and that was the end of that. And that had never happened before.

And at school she was much calmer – she just felt happier in her own skin. She used to chew everything and wear one of those chew toys around her neck, but she started coming home and saying that she hadn't used it today because she hadn't felt as if she needed it. Then she would come home and say that she hadn't taken it out of her bag. She also had stress balls and found that she wasn't needing to use them at all.

Me: So being more regulated on a bodily level, building up those foundation systems, was helping with her emotional regulation?

Mum: Yes, and it's built from there. The big thing we were worried about was her climbing classes. She loves climbing but she can't move up to the next class until she's a year older. So they had put her in another class of children who were like her and showed some promise but were a bit too young. Even though she could do the physical side of it, we would sit and watch her arguing with the instructor the whole time; she was always wanting to be first. We could see that she'd get bored and start to drift off, to the point that they said that if it didn't change, she'd have to move out of that group.

A week after we'd started this programme they came to me and said that she'd had a good week. Then the next week was amazing, and they were saying, 'What is it that's changed?' To me that was incredible.

And school said that she was so much calmer and that they could reason with her, because they had got to the point of saying that when she was in that moment there was just nothing they could do. So we are just keeping going and trying to challenge things more. We can't believe it. My parents say that when she stays at their house, they've noticed that she's just more comfortable in her own skin. The difference is astounding.

Me: That is interesting, because the focus of the intervention is on building bodily regulation, but what you're describing is that alongside the shift in that there is a sense of herself – being able to stay in the moment, manage frustration, not have to be in charge all the time. Those are huge changes.

Mum: She can recognize now how she's feeling and put it into words.

Me: It's lovely to see that capacity growing; it feels as if she's really growing into herself.

Mum: We will just keep going with it all but we are absolutely over the moon!

Elsa

I saw Elsa and her family on the four-stage training, assessment and intervention model at Oakdale. The family worked really hard and were able to come to gym club, which has meant I've been able to stay in touch and watch as Elsa continues to make progress. Elsa's mum has done an amazing job of tracking the changes she's noticed since they've been doing the work to build Elsa's foundation systems. She divided them into 3–6 months post intervention and 6–12 months post-intervention.

3–6 months post-intervention – bodily regulation
Vestibular and proprioceptive systems

- *Sitting* – Elsa is better able to sit on a chair at mealtimes. At home this means she eats much better. At school she finds it much easier to sit and is able to complete tasks. At home she can sit at the table and write her homework really neatly. Elsa is delighted that her letters look the way she'd like them to!

- Elsa recently completed a wood-balancing trail without any help. She would never have been able to do this before.

- Overall walking and running are much smoother and better coordinated. Elsa gets pleasure from moving around and being able to do the things she wants to do.

- Elsa now goes up and down a flight of stairs without using her eyes to track her movements or her hands on the banisters. She comes down putting one foot on each step, and can do this at various speeds.

- She can now do handstands and really good cartwheels. Elsa also loves hula-hooping – these are all things Elsa tried before but just didn't have enough control of her body to be able to do. She's also started learning to roller skate.

Tactile system
Elsa is a much better eater – less fussy and enjoys her food more.

3–6 months post-intervention – emotional regulation

- I've noticed Elsa doing things that she's never been able to do before in terms of understanding herself on an emotional level and being able to regulate. A couple of examples from this week: First, when Elsa gets angry she now asks if she can do some exercise or read a book like her *How Are You Feeling Today?* book. She's got a sense of how she's feeling and that she needs to calm down, and is beginning to be able to do that. The second example happened last week after a crying session where Elsa suddenly said she had tummy ache (she had been fine all evening). She finally managed to tell me that she felt lonely in her bedroom at night and it was too dark. This is the first time she's been able to tell me exactly what she feels.

- Angry outbursts at home have definitely decreased as Elsa is better able to understand herself and how she is feeling. Bedtimes have also got a lot better, both in terms of how long it takes for Elsa to get off to sleep and how much parental intervention is required.

6–12 months post-intervention – bodily regulation
Vestibular and proprioceptive systems

- We had a lovely moment when Elsa brushed my hair gently – she could not have done this before, as it was always much too hard and hurt me.

- Elsa is becoming more confident in her physical abilities. She is very happy in the water at swimming and is progressing well. She loves trampolines and inflatables and talked about enjoying some cricket coaching they are having at school. At the park, she climbs, hangs and balances much more confidently and has tried the zip wire. I feel happier watching her as she is less likely to fall or get stuck somewhere and need rescuing!

- Elsa can now sit on her chair for the whole meal.

- At school, Elsa has struggled with writing and was going into a freeze mode. Supported by her teacher's patience and by her gently grounding her and reminding her what to do, Elsa has been able to get on with her work, complete tasks and write more neatly.

6–12 months post-intervention – emotional regulation

- I've noticed a difference in Elsa being able to 'read' other people's behaviour and signals more clearly and then be able to modify her behaviour. There was an example this week when she cuddled me when she saw she was making me cross – and was satisfied I appreciated it.

- After telling me she was lonely at bedtime, she was much more able to cooperate with a new routine where we will go and check on her after she has gone to bed if she doesn't shout, bang, make a fuss and so on. We now just keep checking until she is asleep.

- With help, Elsa has managed to keep her bedroom quite tidy for over eight weeks. I've noticed that she no longer throws paper on the floor. In general, she is more able to tidy up after herself with help.

- This week when she hurt her sister she apologized and gave her a 'sorry' hug. First time ever!

- Elsa has been much more emotional and anxious and had a particularly tricky time getting back into routine after Christmas, but is more able to tell us what she is feeling. She is also more receptive going back to resources we have which talk about emotions, and doing work with me on anxiety. It's as if she can now take in the information and we can talk about it when a situation arises. It is easier for me to sense how she is feeling as she is more open.

- Elsa is more receptive to therapeutic parenting techniques and over the last two weeks things have been much calmer at home. For example, it is becoming easier and less stressful to get her ready in the morning, although it still takes such a long time and I have to be very patient. We have had much calmer mornings and fewer tears!

Percy's BUSS journey

This is an account from Percy's mother.

Background

Percy came to live with us aged two-and-a-half years. We always had concerns about his gross and fine motor skills. At first he was quite small and a lot of his tripping up and difficulties with coordination, balance and pencil skills could be explained by his young age. But these difficulties continued and were affecting his schooling, particularly his handwriting and reluctance to do anything requiring fine motor skills. He also was teased about his coordination and inability to run alongside his peers. School was a really hard place for him.

He was assessed by Sarah aged eight-and-a-half years.

Assessment

During the assessment process, we saw how underdeveloped Percy's systems were. It was more severe than we realized, and it gave an explanation to so many difficulties that we'd seen him have. It really does affect so many areas of life, not just physical movement but sensitivity to touch, chewing/swallowing difficulties, staying in the moment and so on. We were given some very basic exercises and activities to do such as tummy time, the feely bag game, crawling and commando crawling. These were short activities that we needed to repeat many times a day, every day. At first, Percy found these really tough, but he was enthusiastic (mostly) and he had a personal goal of 'wanting to run faster'. Progress was very slow, and when we met Sarah again a month later, Percy's abilities were not much improved. We were worried by this but carried on with the original plan plus a few new exercises. After six weeks we had a breakthrough, and after this it really snowballed. It was great! As his abilities grew, so did his confidence and we tried even more new or adapted activities to keep his interest. When we saw Sarah for his last assessment, he had made so much progress from where he started. We were so pleased and grateful.

Post-assessment

We have continued with the exercises and activities, but also as Percy now has new abilities for gross and fine movement we are able to use some 'normal activities' to build up his core and upper body strength. He does have setbacks if he is stressed or worried, but we know he can come back from these, and we slip in more of the earlier exercises at these times. We are truly amazed at the things he can now do that most people take for granted, such as running while looking in a different direction, balancing on a scooter, brushing his teeth himself, even simply walking down a flight of stairs without holding on. His handwriting has improved enormously, and he no longer has such reluctance to pick up a pencil and do an activity, because he knows he can do it and be proud. He has more confidence in himself and he fits his body better.

The thing that has been most apparent in this journey is that it has not just been about developing the sensory system. Percy is a whole child, and his sensory system is a part of him. As this has been developed and improved, we have seen a big change in his overall self-esteem, well-being, confidence with his peers socially, academic progress and a general happiness at fitting himself better. This was far more than we hoped for and we are truly thankful.

Before we started the programme, he had:

- very little upper body strength:
  - unable to support his upper body to sit upright for a length of time
  - unable to climb upwards or hold on to anything from above in playgrounds
- very poor posture:
  - walking hunched forwards with head down and leaning forwards
- hypersensitivity:
  - very ticklish
  - sensitive to texture/temperatures

- very poor balance and bodily awareness:
  - unable to ride a bike without looking where his feet were
  - holding on to walk down the stairs
  - struggling to walk and carry a plate/drink
  - regularly tripping/falling
- very poor whole-body coordination:
  - 'swimming' below water (unable to do arm and leg movements together)
  - difficulty running/playing football
- some difficulties with chewing, knowing when to drink, swallowing reflex
- extremely poor fine motor skills:
  - terrible handwriting/pencil control
  - struggling with Lego®/small toys
  - unable to brush teeth properly.

These all led to low self-esteem, low confidence, upset, reluctance to try/participate, isolation from peers, teasing in playground, and he tired easily from any physical exertion. School was really hard!

We were originally referred to a regular NHS occupational therapist. They agreed that it wasn't a sensory processing disorder but was due to his early life situation, and that 'he would get there eventually'. The advice they offered made little difference. We now know this was because it did not address the early developmental gaps he had. You can't build on something that isn't there to start with. All Percy wanted was 'to be able to run faster'.

His initial assessment with Sarah showed that he:

- couldn't commando crawl at all
- struggled to normally crawl – overcompensating with speed, but his arms and legs did not work together

- couldn't hold himself up well enough to do basic tummy time
- couldn't hold a prone extension position at all.

We were back to basics with high repetition of exercises every day. Percy was compliant and enthusiastic (mostly), even though some of it was very hard for him.

We didn't see much improvement for about six weeks. It was very slow going and we were worried, but then there was a huge leap of improvement all at once. It was a snowball effect – as his abilities grew, so did his confidence. Six months on, what an amazing difference! He now:

- gets on a bike, looks forwards and rides off confidently
- happily runs around and plays tig
- attempts monkey bars in a playground and will persist and try and get further instead of giving up
- has better posture, both sitting and standing
- can tolerate touch more, although I think he will always be ticklish
- is more confident on stairs
- trips over much less
- has much better balance – he has stood on a kayak on water, completed a high ropes course really well, does tricks on a scooter balanced on one leg
- has *much* improved handwriting
- is overall a more confident boy who seems happier in his body.

There is still a way to go, but he is on the right track. This is much more than just physical help, it benefits self-esteem, confidence, socializing, attachment, regulation and education.

Thank you, Sarah! This has changed his life!

Top tips

- Buy a superhero cape to encourage prone extension positions (like Superman or Batman).

- Try lying across a gym ball as an alternative for Superman/ Batman (also good for watching TV).

- Use the thin straws that come with small cartons of juice.

- Try some friendly competition from an older sibling (closely supervised) as a motivator.

- Search for objects in a very bubbly bath as an alternative to the feely bag game.

- Play a daily 'toast taste' game with different toppings on small pieces of toast.

- Do tummy time while watching TV and wrapped up in a blanket or covered up with cushions.

- Do a bug walk or crawl while balancing a teddy/pyjamas on tummy/back.

- Set up a Maltesers® obstacle course, or pick up Maltesers® by sucking them through a straw and moving them from one dish to another.

Percy's favourite things

- Drinking Angel Delight® through a straw (use plastic rather than paper straws unless you want a soggy mess).

- Being Superdog and crawling around the house in character.

- Dabbing (just like Usain Bolt) in a prone extension position.

- Making underwater volcanoes (blowing bubbles in a bath/ bottle).

- Having the Jack Russell dog commando crawling alongside him.

Chapter 18

Final Thoughts

I HOPE that you will have found this book useful, whether you're a parent, carer or practitioner working with children who have experienced developmental trauma. As you will have worked out, I am passionate about bringing an understanding of the role that movement within a loving, nurturing relationship plays in the development of bodily regulation. This then sets the stage for emotional regulation and developing relationships which in turn facilitate good learning. I want families and professionals working with children who have experienced developmental trauma to embrace the idea of these systems being underdeveloped rather than broken, and that families are the best people to help their children grow into themselves on a bodily level. As you'll have gathered from the accounts of parents, the changes that this brings on an emotional and relationship level are fantastic and, in some cases, quite life-changing. Intervening at an early stage of a child's life in the care system and working with families around those underdeveloped systems could save, in emotional terms, so much heartache and missed opportunities, and in financial terms, money being spent on therapies that don't take into account the role that body regulation has to play on an individual's well-being.

When to stop

This is another, 'how long is a piece of string' question. For some children, an initial burst of activities over the first month or so will be enough to get their foundation systems to a level where they can continue to develop just by doing the normal play and outdoor activities of childhood. At that point, the child will have gained good core stability, know where their body is and have smooth and well-coordinated movement, and they can take part in all of the activities of childhood, like having fun at the play park. This will be enough for their systems to grow.

For other children and families, it takes longer to work their way up the different ladders of activities to get to that point. By the time I say goodbye to families, I want them to feel confident in what they're doing and to have lots of ideas about moving forward. I've set up a BUSS gym club, which allows me to stay in touch with families whose progress is slower, for much longer, which is great. It is a fantastic forum for children to continue to develop and for parents to meet and support each other. It would be great to develop a network of these around the country; they are a fantastic way to build a child's foundation systems enough to enable them to take part successfully in a mainstream club.

Generally, I suggest to families that they keep going with some of the games and activities over the next few months, focusing on whatever has been most important for their child's progress. For some, that will be those magic three, of tummy time, commando crawling and crawling (in one form or another!). For others, it will be important to keep going with the games for the tactile system.

I hope that parents will feel confident to make those decisions themselves and to know that, if things start to change, they can pick up the games and activities again. Lenny, who you may remember as the little boy who chewed his way through eight coats in the first terms of school, had a resurgence of chewing things a couple of years later. After a brief chat with me, his mum thought she'd go back and redo lots of the blowing, sucking and tasting games that had helped first time round, and, sure enough, it settled again. Once it had settled, Lenny and his mum were able to talk about what had been making him feel like that and think of ways that she and school were able to support him.

The progress that children like Elsa, Sean, Nadia, Amber, Percy and so many others have been able to make in such a short time is entirely down to the efforts of their parents and carers in making it fun and engaging. For me, the role of the BUSS model is to help families understand the idea of systems being underdeveloped because of early experience, to give information about development and ideas and support for rebuilding these systems. We need practitioners who are trained in using the model and I would love it to be widely available to all children with developmental trauma as a first step in any intervention. But without the thoughtful, playful work of parents and carers, and, in the best cases, schools, nothing will change.

What is so lovely to see is that although the model focuses on bodily regulation, the relationships between parents/carers and their children really grow. Sometimes I think that there's something liberating for foster carers and adoptive parents about shifting the emphasis from attachment and trauma to the possibilities of development. But just as the blueprint of typical development shows us, regulation is built through relationships, just as relationships are built through regulation.

Bibliography

I find that reference lists can sometimes feel a bit impenetrable, so I've divided things into subsections that I hope might make things feel more accessible. I've included a range of printed and web resources as well as a couple of films.

A neurodevelopmental understanding of the impact of early adversity on development

Bear, M.F., Connors, B.W. and Paradiso, A. (2006) *Neuroscience: Exploring the Brain*. Baltimore, MD: Lippincott, Williams and Wilkins.

In Brief: The Impact of Early Adversity on Children's Development. Available at: www.developingchild.harvard.edu/library.

Lane, S.J. and Schaaf, R.C. (2010) 'Examining the neuroscience evidence for sensory-driven neuroplasticity: Implications for sensory-based occupational therapy for children and adolescents.' *American Journal of Occupational Therapy*, 64, 375–390. https://doi.org/10.5014/ajot.2010.09069.

Perry, B. (2006) *The Boy Who Was Raised as a Dog*. New York, NY: Basic Books.

Porges, D. and Dana, D. (2018) *Clinical Applications of Polyvagal Theory*. New York, NY: W.W. Norton.

Szalavitz, M. and Perry, B. (2010) *Born for Love: Why Empathy is Essential – And Endangered*. New York, NY: HarperCollins.

Child development

Frick, S., Frick, R., Oetter, P. and Richter, E. (1996) *Out of the Mouths of Babes*. Stillwater, MN: Pileated Press.

Leadsom, A., Field, F., Burstow, P. and Lucas, C. (2013) *The 1001 Critical Days: The Importance of the Conception to Age Two Period: A Cross Party Manifesto*. Available at: www.1001criticaldays.co.uk.

Sharma, A. and Cockerill, H. (2014a) *Mary Sheridan's from Birth to Five Years: Children's Developmental Progress*. London: Routledge

Sharma, A. and Cockerill, H. (2014b) *From Birth to Five Years Practical Developmental Examination*. London: Routledge.

Stern, D.N. (1985) *The Interpersonal World of the Infant: A View from Psychoanalysis and Developmental Psychology*. New York, NY: Basic Books.

Assessments

Boxall Profile. Available at: https://boxallprofile.org.

Dunn, W. (2014) *Sensory Profile 2*. Bloomington, MN: Pearson. Available at: www.pearsonclinical.co.uk.

Golding, K. (n.d.) 'Thinking about your child' questionnaire. Available at: ddpnetwork.org/library/thinking-child.

Parks, S. (1994) *HELP Curriculum Based Assessment: Birth to 3 Years*. Available at: www.vort.com.

Building underdeveloped sensorimotor systems

Conkbayir, M. (2017) *Early Childhood and Neuroscience: Theory, Research and Implications for Practice*. London and Oxford: Bloomsbury Academic.

Lloyd, S. (2016) *Improving Sensory Processing in Traumatised Children*. London and Philadelphia, PA: Jessica Kingsley Publishers.

Stewart, N. (2011) *How Children Learn: The Characteristics of Effective Early Learning*. Watford: British Association for Early Childhood Education.

Tredgett, S. (2015) *Learning through Movement in the Early Years*. Northwich: Critical Publishing.

Attachment and building relationships

Booth, P. (2009) *Theraplay: Helping Parents and Children Build Better Relationships through Attachment-Based Play*. San Francisco, CA: Jossey-Bass.

Bhreathnach, E. (2011) *The Scared Gang*. Belfast: Alder Tree Press.

Garvey, D. (2018) *Nurturing Personal, Social and Emotional Development in Early Childhood: A Practical Guide to Understanding Brain Development and Young Children's Behaviour*. London and Philadelphia, PA: Jessica Kingsley Publishers.

Gerhardt, S. (2004, reprinted 2014) *Why Love Matters: How Affection Shapes a Baby's Brain*. London: Routledge.

Golding, K. (n.d.) 'Thinking about your child' questionnaire. Available at: ddpnetwork.org/library/thinking-child.

Golding, K. and Hughes, D. (2012) *Creating Loving Attachments: Parenting with PACE to Nurture Confidence and Security in the Troubled Child*. London and Philadelphia, PA: Jessica Kingsley Publishers.

Greenberg, M., Cicchetti, D. and Cummings E.M. (1990) *Attachment in the Preschool Years*. Chicago, IL: The University of Chicago Press.

Guerney, L. and Ryan, V. (2013) *Group Filial Therapy: The Complete Guide to Teaching Parents to Play Therapeutically with Their Children*. London and Philadelphia, PA: Jessica Kingsley Publishers.

Hughes, D. and Baylin, J. (2012) *Brain-Based Parenting: The Science of Caregiving for Healthy Attachment*. New York, NY: W.W. Norton.

Hughes, D.A., Golding, K.S. and Hudson, J. (2019) *Healing Relational Trauma with Attachment Focused Interventions*. New York, NY: W.W. Norton.

Malloch, S. and Trevarthen, C. (2010) *Communicative Musicality: Exploring the Basis of Human Companionship*. Oxford: Oxford University Press.

Murray, L. and Andrews, L. (2000) *The Social Baby*. Richmond, Surrey: CP Publishing.

Music, G. (2011) *Nurturing Natures: Attachment and Children's Emotional, Sociocultural and Brain Development*. Hove, East Sussex: Psychology Press.

Patchett, A. (2017) *Run*. London: Bloomsbury Publishing.

Stern, D.N. (1985) *The Interpersonal World of the Infant: A View from Psychoanalysis and Developmental Psychology*. New York, NY: Basic Books.

Treisman, K. (2006) *Working with Relational and Developmental Trauma in Children and Adolescents*. London: Routledge.

Trevarthen, C. Delafield-Butt, J. and Dunlop, A-W. (2018) *The Child's Curriculum: Working with the Natural Valurs of Your Children.* Oxford: Oxford University Press.

VanFleet, R. (2013) *Filial Therapy: Strengthening Parent–Child Relationships through Play.* Sarasota, FL: Professional Resource Press.

Winnicott, D. (1957/1964) *The Child, the Family and the Outside World.* London: Penguin Books.

Zeedyk, S. (2011) *The Connected Baby.* A documentary film produced by Dr Suzanne Zeedyk, a developmental psychologist based at the University of Dundee, Scotland. The film-maker was Jonathan Robertson.

Sensory integration and children with sensory processing disorders

Ayres, A.J. (2005) (25th anniversary edition) *Sensory Integration and the Child: Understanding Hidden Sensory Challenges.* Los Angeles, CA: Western Psychological Services.

Biel, L. and Peske, N. (2009) *Raising a Sensory Smart Child: The Definitive Handbook for Helping Your Child with Sensory Processing Issues.* New York, NY: Penguin Books.

Brown, K. (2012) *Educate Your Brain: Use Mind–Body Balance to Learn Faster, Work Smarter and Move Through Life More Easily.* Phoenix, AZ: Balance Point Publishing LLC.

DeGangi, G. (2000) *Pediatric Disorders of Regulation in Affect and Behaviour: A Therapist's Guide to Assessment and Treatment.* London: Academic Press Limited.

Horwood, J. (2008) *Sensory Circuits: A Sensory Motor Skills Programme for Children.* Cambridge: LDA.

Kocsinski, C. (2017) *Sensorimotor Interventions.* Arlington, TX; Future Horizon Incorporated.

Kranowitz, C. (2005) *The Out of Synch Child.* New York, NY: Penguin Books.

Kranowitz, C. and Newman, J. (2010) *Growing an In-Synch Child: Simple, Fun Activities to Help Every Child Develop, Learn and Grow.* New York, NY: Penguin Books.

Other internet resources

Beacon House: a fantastic collection of brilliant resources, information and advice for children, families and schools – http://beaconhouse.org.uk.

Beacon House YouTube clip on 'Window of Tolerance' can be found at www.you tube.com/watch?v=Wcm-1FBrDvU.

ChildTrauma Academy – http://childtrauma.org.

Perry, B.D. (The ChildTrauma Academy) (2013) '1: The Human Brain' (video webcast). In *Seven Slide Series*. Available at: www.youtube.com/watch?v=uOsgDkeH52o.

Polyvagal theory: Ruby Jo Walker has a great website in which she manages to bring together the essence of polyvagal theory but in a very simple form – www.rubyjowalker.com.

Sensory Attachment Intervention website, outlining the work of Eadaoin Bhreathnach – www.sensoryattachmentintervention.com.

The Wrong Trousers. Wallace and Gromit film, produced by Aardman Animations in 2015 – www.wallaceandgromit.com.

There are a few websites developed by paediatric occupational therapists that very nicely illustrate typical development and offer some guidance for parents who have concerns about aspects of their child's development. At the time of publication, my two favourites and the ones I've referred to in the text are https://mamaOT.com and www.candokiddo.com.

For younger children

These are lovely stories and also feature lots of animals – great for all that crawling, commando crawling and bear walking!

Campbell, R. (2010) *Dear Zoo*. London: Macmillan Publications.

Carle, E. (1994) *The Very Hungry Caterpillar*. New York, NY: Puffin Books.

Donaldson, J. (2017) *The Gruffalo*. London: Macmillan Publications.

Donaldson, J. (2018) *The Snail and the Whale*. London: Macmillan Publications.

Donaldson, J. (2017) *A Squash and a Squeeze*. London: Macmillan Publications.

Rose, M. (2015) *We're Going on a Bear Hunt*. London: Walker Books.

Voake, C. (2008) *Ginger*. London: Walker Books.

Subject Index

Author Index

By the same author

Improving Sensory Processing in Traumatized Children
Practical Ideas to Help Your Child's Movement, Coordination and Body Awareness

Paperback: £9.99 / $16.95
ISBN: 978 1 78592 004 2
eISBN: 978 1 78450 239 3
120 pages

Does your child struggle to know how their body is feeling? Do they find it hard to balance or feel uneasy when their feet leave the ground?

Early trauma and neglect can have a profound effect upon a child's development. Sensory integration theory offers a way of understanding how the brain processes and stores movement experience, and how these experiences manifest at a physical and emotional level. This book explains how early movement experiences affect brain development and gives examples of how trauma can prevent basic sensory processing pathways from being correctly established. It shows how you can identify gaps in normal sensory development and offers ideas for how you can use physical activities to help build up the underdeveloped systems. Good bodily awareness forms the foundation of motor development as well as social and emotional skills and learning. This book will help your child to be more in tune with themselves and their bodies and feel more comfortable in their environment.

Highly accessible with lots of practical tips and examples, this book is written for adoptive and foster parents, and will also be useful for social workers, fostering and adoption workers and those working in primary and early years educational settings.

Of related interest

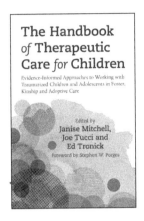

The Handbook
of Therapeutic
Care for Children
Evidence-Informed Approaches to Working with
Traumatized Children and Adolescents in Foster,
Kinship and Adoptive Care

Edited by
Janise Mitchell,
Joe Tucci and
Ed Tronick
foreword by Stephen W. Porges

The Handbook of Therapeutic Care for Children
Evidence-Informed Approaches
to Working with Traumatized
Children and Adolescents in Foster,
Kinship and Adoptive Care
Edited by Janise Mitchell, Joe Tucci and Ed Tronick

Paperback: £29.99 / $42.95
ISBN: 978 1 78592 751 5
eISBN: 978 1 78450 554 7
336 pages

This innovative book brings together a wide range of therapeutic approaches, techniques and models to outline recent developments in the practice of supporting children in out-of-home care. It sheds light on the significance of schools, sports and peer relationships in the lives of traumatized children. It also draws particular attention to the vital importance of taking into account children's cultural heritage, and to the growing prevalence of relative care.

Each chapter is set out by acclaimed and world-renowned contributors' specific approach, such as Dan Hughes and his work on conceptual maps and Cathy Malchiodi and her research on creative interventions, and gives practical ways to support children and carers. It also includes contributions from Bruce Perry, Allan Schore and Martin Teicher. This comprehensive volume will open new avenues for understanding how the relationship between child and carer can create opportunities for change and healing.

Janise Mitchell is Deputy CEO of the Australian Childhood Foundation, a social worker and a children's rights advocate.

Joe Tucci is CEO of the Australian Childhood Foundation, a social worker, a psychologist and a children's rights advocate.

Ed Tronick is Distinguished University Professor of Psychology, College of Liberal Arts and Director of Child Development Unit at the University of Massachusetts.

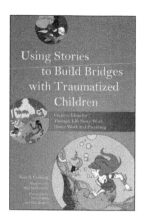

Using Stories to Build Bridges with Traumatized Children
Creative Ideas for Therapy, Life Story Work, Direct Work and Parenting
Kim S. Golding

Paperback: £16.99 / $27.95
ISBN: 978 1 84905 540 6
eISBN: 978 0 85700 961 6
176 pages

Using Stories to Build Bridges with Traumatized Children is full of creative ideas for how you can use stories therapeutically with children in counselling, life story work or direct work.

Psychologist Kim S. Golding shows how you can use stories to build connections with children aged 4–16 and support their recovery from trauma and stress. She illustrates the techniques with 21 stories adapted from her own clinical work with children and families, and explains how you can expand or adapt them to make them more relevant for a particular child. Advice and stories are arranged into sections dealing with common psychological issues, including looking back and moving on, lack of trust and need for attention. Golding also gives invaluable tips for planning stories and life story work, and for storymaking with children. She also describes how stories can be used therapeutically with parents of traumatized children and as a tool for self-reflection by counsellors.

Kim S. Golding is a clinical psychologist who works in Worcestershire, England where she was influential in the founding of the Integrated Service for Looked After Children – a multi-agency, holistic service providing support for foster, adoptive and residential parents, schools and the range of professionals supporting children growing up in care or in adoptive families. Kim was trained and mentored by Dan Hughes in the use of Dyadic Developmental Psychotherapy (DDP). She accredits and trains professionals in the approach in the UK and has been invited to speak about this work internationally. She is the author of a number of books on attachment, adoption and fostering, including *Creating Loving Attachments: Parenting with PACE to Nurture Confidence and Security in the Troubled Child*, co-authored with Dan Hughes and published by Jessica Kingsley Publishers.

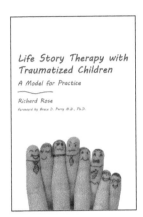

Life Story Therapy with Traumatized Children
A Model for Practice
Richard Rose

Paperback: £22.99 / $32.95
ISBN: 978 1 84905 272 6
eISBN: 978 0 85700 574 8
192 pages

Life Story Therapy is an approach designed to enable children to explore, question and understand the past events of their lives. It aims to secure their future through strengthening attachment with their carers and providing the opportunity to develop a healthy sense of self and a feeling of wellbeing.

This comprehensive overview lays out the theory underlying life story therapy, including an accessible explanation of contemporary research in neurobiology and trauma. Featuring tried and tested ideas, with tools and templates illustrated through instructive case studies, the author identifies how life story therapy can be implemented in practice. Finally, the relationships between life story therapy and traditional 'talking' therapies are explored.

Life Story Therapy with Traumatized Children is essential reading for those working with children and adolescents, including social workers, teachers, child psychotherapists, residential care staff, long-term carers, psychologists and other professionals.

Richard Rose is the Director of Child Trauma Intervention Services Ltd and an Adjunct Associate Professor of Social Work and Social Policy at La Trobe University, Melbourne, Australia. He is also a Fellow of the Berry Street Childhood Institute, part of Berry Street, Australia and Lead Consultant for Clinical Practice at SACCS, UK. He undertakes consultancy and training on Life Story Therapy and working with 'hard to reach' children and adolescents, and develops academic training programmes in the UK and internationally. He is co-author of *The Child's Own Story: Life Story Work with Traumatized Children*.

Attachment-Based
Milieus for Healing Child
and Adolescent
Developmental Trauma
A RELATIONAL APPROACH FOR USE IN
SETTINGS FROM INPATIENT PSYCHIATRY
TO SPECIAL EDUCATION CLASSROOMS
FOREWORD BY DAN HUGHES

Attachment-Based Milieus for Healing Child and Adolescent Developmental Trauma
A Relational Approach for Use in Settings from Inpatient Psychiatry to Special Education Classrooms
John Stewart

Hardback ISBN: 978 1 78592 789 8
Paperback ISBN: 978 1 78592 790 4
eISBN: 978 1 78450 739 8
216 pages

This book presents an innovative relational and community based therapeutic model to ensure children's essential attachment needs are catered for in intensive mental health care.

The text combines an overview of theory relating to attachment and trauma before laying out a model for working with children and adolescents in an attachment-informed way. The approach applies to a diverse range of settings - from in-patient psychiatric settings, through to schools-based programs, and provides the reader with the knowledge and guidance they need to introduce the approach in their own service. It also addresses the complexities of working with specific clinical populations, including children with ADHD, ASD, RAD and psychosis.

Accessible for entry level clinical caretakers, yet sophisticated enough for clinical supervisors, this book is essential reading for professionals looking to improve the effectiveness of child and adolescent treatment programs.

John Stewart is a psychologist with 35 years' experience. He is Assistant Clinical Professor, Department of Psychiatry, Tufts School of Medicine, Boston MA.